WHY IS IT ALWAYS ABOUT **YOU** **?**

The Seven Deadly Sins
of Narcissism

Sandy Hotchkiss, LCSW

FREE PRESS

NEW YORK   LONDON   TORONTO   SYDNEY

FREE PRESS
A Division of Simon & Schuster, Inc.
1230 Avenue of the Americas
New York, NY 10020

First FREE PRESS trade paperback edition 2003

FREE PRESS and colophon are trademarks
of Simon & Schuster Inc.

Designed by Jan Pisciotta

Manufactured in the United States of America

7   9   10   8

Library of Congress Cataloging-in-Publication Data

Hotchkiss, Sandy
Why is it always about you? the seven deadly sins of narcissism /
Sandy Hotchkiss.
p. cm.
Includes bibliographical references (p.) and index.
l. Narcissism   I. Title
BF575H68   2002
158.2—dc21   2-1-54516

ISBN 0-7432-1427-7
0-7432-1428-5 (Pbk)

For information regarding special discounts for bulk purchases,
please contact Simon & Schuster Special Sales at 1-800-456-6798
or business@simonandschuster.com

For Donald
Ever "a friend to my excitement"

ACKNOWLEDGMENTS

This book was in my head for five years before I began putting it on paper, and many people have nurtured it along the way.

I wish to thank my patients, who confirmed my belief that a book about why Narcissists act the way they do had a place in the world. Their struggles to extricate themselves from the webs cast by narcissistic parents, lovers, spouses, bosses, and friends made psychoanalytic theory come alive for me and showed me how it is possible to develop a whole and separate Self beyond childhood. I am particularly grateful to those who gave permission for me to share their stories in these pages.

I also wish to thank all of my professional colleagues who supported me when I decided to cancel my managed-care contracts in late 1997. Giving up more than half of my practice created the time to write this book, but it also meant a loss of income. I am fortunate to be part of a community that has helped me keep my doors open through a very tumultuous time in the history of psychotherapy, when managed care has taken control of the therapy process and threatens the very essence of what we do that is helpful.

Thanks, too, to my wonderful husband, Donald Hildreth, who dragged me from the dark ages of legal pads and ballpoint pens, electric typewriters and Wite-Out, to the joys of the word processor. I wrote the first several chapters of this book sitting back-to-back with him in his art studio, me at his computer and he at his easel, in the *feng shui* corner of our house. Ultimately, he bought me my own little laptop, and a whole new world opened up. Thank you for bringing me into the light, and for always being the light of my life.

This book could not have been conceived, let alone published, without the significant contributions of James Masterson, M.D. I discovered the Masterson Approach to treating Disorders of the Self in 1987, and his clear, sound, and utterly relevant model has been the foundation of my clinical work throughout my career. In early 2000, he generously agreed to read portions of the manuscript and ultimately opened the door for me at Simon & Schuster. That he was also willing to write my Foreword is an honor I will treasure for a lifetime.

Writing this book has brought me in closer contact with many delightful people who have each been instrumental as the journey unfolded. Topping the list is my dear friend and colleague Suzanne Lake, Psy.D., who read every draft of the manuscript, offering tireless encouragement through countless anxious moments. My agent, Peter Fleming, will always be dear to me as the first person from the literary world to express enthusiasm about my ideas. Elizabeth Knowles of Harvard Press and Kitty Moore at Guilford generously gave time and feedback on early drafts. Emily Brown, LCSW, has been a model and an advisor. Aileen Berg, a gift from heaven, provided the essential link to ultimate publication. And my stepson, Jeremy Hildreth, made it happen with the "Only You Can Prevent Narcissism" T-shirt that brought Aileen and me together. What serendipity!

Thanks also go to Kathy Coss, Colleen Garner, Carol Schwartz, and Whitney Wagner for their impressions of early drafts of the manuscript. Thank you, moms and girlfriends!

My experience at The Free Press has been wonderful from the outset. Thanks so much to Trish Todd, who listened to her friend Aileen Berg and passed my proposal on to Philip Rappaport, who has been a sweetheart of an editor. Immersing oneself in narcissism can activate anger, and Philip's kindness and optimism helped me keep my balance through the revision process. Thanks also to Philip's able assistant Elizabeth Haymaker for putting my manuscript on disk.

Contents

Part IV: "Special People": The Narcissists in Your Life

Part V: Only You Can Prevent Narcissism

CONTENTS

FOREWORD

People who are involved in business and/or close relationships with people who have Narcissistic Personality Disorder are often bewildered and perplexed by the extraordinary contradictions of their behavior, in contrast to the underlying enduring consistency of their narcissistic needs. These needs are expressed in their grandiose search for constant admiration, underneath which lies an exquisite vulnerability to the slightest rebuff, which then evokes devastating shame. Their behavior can be charismatic and charming one minute, cold and calculating the next, or on occasion breaking into unpredictable rages.

I have often seen this bewilderment in the parents, spouses, and children of patients in treatment. They cannot believe what their perception is telling them: that the patient is caught in the unvarying cycle of narcissistic vulnerability and defense.

I have long wished we had a book that provides an understanding of the cyclical vicissitudes of this problem, as well as the possibilities offered by treatment.

At last we do have such a book: *Why Is It Always About You?* by Sandy Hotchkiss, LCSW. This book is beautifully written and a pleasure to read. Ms. Hotchkiss has marshaled and integrated the considerable professional literature on the subject and translated it into plain English for the lay reader. Highly technical concepts are explained and concretely illustrated in detail. Excellent references are noted with each chapter. This volume fills a vast void in the literature and is a must-read for anyone, whether a professional or a layperson, seeking a better understanding of the Narcissistic Personality Disorder.

James F. Masterson, M.D.

Director, Masterson Institute for Psychoanalytic Psychotherapy

Emeritus Professor of Psychiatry

Cornell University Medical College, New York Hospital

They're Everywhere

IT'S A QUARTER TILL FIVE, and you've had one of those days at work. The phones have been ringing nonstop, lunch was a whiff of pizza wafting down from the employee lounge, and everyone seems to have wanted a piece of *you* to chew on. But despite the interruptions, you've been able to finish that report that's been hanging over your head for the past week. As you feel yourself winding down, you look over your phone messages and start to prioritize what you'll tackle tomorrow. Your thoughts begin to drift to a good meal, a hot soak in the tub, and an early bedtime.

Suddenly, your reverie is punctured by a head poking into your cubicle. "The big guy needs us to run these numbers again," your coworker says, dropping a stack of papers on your desk. "Sorry I can't stay to help—Judy and I have theater tickets." Not again, you think. Why does this always happen at the last minute, and why am I the one who usually gets stuck staying late?

An hour later, you climb into your car and head for home. At a stop sign, you wait while three teenagers slowly shuffle across the street, oblivious to the cars in every direction. Could they go any slower? You tap your horn politely, hoping to jolt them into picking up the pace. They continue their leisurely stroll, one of them snarling an obscenity as he passes by. Kids. When did they become so hostile?

Home at last, you walk in the door and see your husband relaxing in front of the evening news, a beer in hand and two empties on the coffee table. "You're late," he calls out. "What's for dinner?" "Leftovers," you yell back, relieved that there's something edible in the fridge. "I've been craving fried chicken all day," he says, petulantly. "You could cook a decent meal for a guy every once in a while." Or *you* could pay a call on the Colonel, you mutter under your breath.

Later, while you're washing the dishes, the phone rings. It's your mother. "You haven't called me in three days," she says as soon as she hears your voice. "Hi, Mom, how ya doin'?" you reply. "Not good, not good. I'm out of milk, my check needs to be deposited, and the darned cleaning lady didn't show up again. If I had a daughter who cared about anything besides her career, I wouldn't have to hire people to do these things for me." And if I had a mother, a voice inside you says, maybe there would be someone who gave a rip how *my* day has gone.

Ten P.M. Your big, cozy bed beckons. You climb into your old flannel jammies and crawl, at last, into its king-sized embrace. But your day is not quite over. "Honey," your husband says, pulling you close and nuzzling your neck, "why don't you put on that nightie I gave you for your birthday?" Earth to hubby—do I look like I'm in the mood?

Sometimes it seems as if the world is full of selfish people who have no thought for others except how to use them for their own purposes. Their needs are more important than anyone else's, and they expect to be accommodated in all things. They can't seem to see the bigger picture, or to comprehend why they might not always come first. Their expectations have an almost childlike quality, yet they can be tyrannically outraged or pitifully depressed when thwarted. Often, we give in to them because it seems safer not to rock their boat.

We all know people like this. They may be our parents, siblings, or children; our spouses, lovers, and friends; our coworkers and bosses; the people we get to know through the clubs and organizations we belong to. They are everywhere, and the more intertwined our lives are with theirs, the more miserable we feel.

That misery is a byproduct of a personality flaw that, by cultural standards, has become disturbingly "normal." We sense that something is wrong but can't quite put our finger on what it is. We see it in our daily dealings with one another, which in many cases have become less kind, courteous, or inclined toward generosity. We feel it in our workplaces, which are permeated with resentment, anxiety, and debilitating job-related stress. But perhaps the place where we are most affected is in those intimate relationships with friends, lovers, and family that give life its richness and meaning. By its very nature, this sickness isolates us from one another and from reality, and it stands between us and all that we can hope to have and be. Its name is narcissism, and it lurks behind many of the social ills that plague twenty-first-century America.

There is nothing new about narcissism. There have always been vain, grasping, manipulative characters who have an inflated perception of themselves and little regard for others. What is troubling about contemporary culture is the extent to which these personality flaws have received a widespread stamp of approval. Narcissism is not just tolerated in our day and age, it is glorified. Many of our leaders and the public figures we admire flaunt their narcissistic proclivities, and we can't wait to emulate their excesses. On them, outrageous behavior looks glamorous and exciting, so we give ourselves permission to share in the "fun." Before we know it, the distinction between what's healthy and what isn't gets fuzzy, and "Everybody does it" becomes the justification for continuing down the path.

Back in the mid-1970s, the sociologist Christopher Lasch wrote a book called *The Culture of Narcissism* that made a lot of people think about what had been going on in American society since the end of World War II. He discussed the feelings of omnipotence, prosperity, and security that had characterized our national spirit in the 1950s, reaching an apex in the "Camelot" days of the Kennedy administration.

Things began to shift when a young and much-idealized president was cut down by an assassin's bullet, just as the first wave of baby boomers hit the shores of adolescence. A tsunami of youthful confusion and experimentation engulfed the culture, even as America began to grapple with other disasters. In the next fifteen years, economic stagnation, defeat in Vietnam, and the impending exhaustion of natural resources created a mood of pessimism. In an "Age of Diminishing Expectations," wrote Lasch, the rosy glow on the horizon had dimmed.

While the "can-do" spirit of the 1950s and 1960s had yielded unprecedented advances in science and technology, these achievements ultimately proved insufficient to bring about the political and social reforms that an increasingly youth-dominated culture aspired to in the late 1960s. Lasch described how we came to despair of changing society and began to turn inward, focusing on the only thing we could hope to control, ourselves. Through expanded consciousness, health, and personal growth, we sought to soothe our anxiety about an uncertain world. We became, in a sense, preoccupied with "Self."

For all our anxious preoccupation, however, we seem to have a love-hate relationship with the very notion of "Self." Sometimes it is associated with undesirable qualities such as selfishness, egotism, and conceit. On the other hand, "selflessness" also raises our suspicions. If someone is overly invested in caring for others, we call them codependent and tell them to start putting themselves first. Martyrdom is distinctly out of style. But when we hyphenate the word Self and add "awareness" or "esteem," Self becomes downright positive.

Is Self good or is it bad? It would not be possible to function, let alone survive, without some degree of investment in the Self. Without attention to ourselves, we would remain undeveloped and unaware, our talents lying dormant and our values unformed. In a world without ego, there would be no originality, no color, no contrast. Variety would cease to exist, and choice would become unnecessary. Even love would be meaningless if there were no "I" to be smitten with "you."

Healthy narcissism, the investment of energy in one's genuine Self, has primitive roots in infancy and early childhood and blossoms into full flower in an emotionally rich, productive, and satisfying adult life. It is healthy narcissism that allows us to laugh at ourselves and our imperfections, to dig deep within ourselves to create something uniquely ours, and to leave a positive personal stamp on the world. Healthy narcissism is the capacity to feel a full range of emotions and to share in the emotional life of others, the wisdom to separate truth from fantasy while still being able to dream, and the ability to assertively pursue and enjoy our own accomplishments without crippling self-doubt. Healthy narcissism depends on real self-esteem, which is something completely lacking in the people we commonly describe as Narcissists.

The Narcissist we recognize as unhealthy is someone who, no matter what age, has not yet fully developed emotionally or morally. This person lacks a realistic sense of Self and an internalized system of values—apart from unmitigated self-interest—that guides behavior. In place of an accurate assessment of personal strengths, there is an exaggerated posture of importance unrelated to any real accomplishments. Instead of humility in the face of inevitable shortcomings, there is an overwhelming, and utterly intolerable, sense of shame, though this is often well-disguised. There is also no ability to value, or often enough even to recognize, the separate existence or feelings of other people. The Narcissist may be intimidating, mesmerizing, even larger-than-life, but beneath the bombast or the charm is an emotional cripple with the moral development of a toddler.

The characteristic ways that Narcissists think and behave are what I describe in Part I as the Seven Deadly Sins. Some of these, such as entitlement and the rage that accompanies it, arrogance, and magical thinking (grandiosity and omnipotence) are familiar faces of narcissism. But you may be surprised to learn that poor interpersonal boundaries, the emotional shallowness that stems from buried shame, envy and its sidekick contempt, and the exploitiveness that fills the vacuum created by the absence of empathy are even more indicative of unhealthy narcissism than an inflated ego or mere selfishness. These are the behavior and attitudes that protect an undeveloped Self at the expense of the well-being of others. They are deadly because they invade and annihilate the integrity of everyone they touch, and sinful because they destroy the sinner as well. The Seven Deadly Sins of Narcissism not only hurt others, but they prevent the Narcissist from developing a genuine Self.

To begin to understand how to protect yourself from the Narcissists you encounter in your life, it is useful to know who you are dealing with and how they came to be the way they are. In Part II, you will learn that narcissism is a normal stage we all pass through in early childhood on our way to becoming more complete human beings. To make the transition, we need the help of healthy parents who have their own unhealthy narcissism in reasonable check and are capable of nurturing individuality in their children while teaching values and respect for others. When parents are themselves narcissistic, they often use their children in self-serving ways and fail to guide them to a healthy resolution of normal childhood narcissism. The result is another generation of Narcissists—as well as people who seem to be magnets for this personality type.

In Part III, you will learn four survival strategies for defending your Self against the damage that Narcissists can do. The first step is to identify whatever vulnerabilities have been carried forward from your past. The more you were exposed to parental narcissism as a child, the more sensitive you may be to the Narcissists you encounter in the present. While Narcissists tend to beget Narcissists, such parents also raise children who are the mirror image of narcissism—more shame-sensitive than shameless, more covert in their hunger for recognition, more likely to be exploited than to exploit, but just as confused about personal boundaries. This confusion, along with their difficulty in asserting themselves, makes them easy prey for the Narcissists who will continue to use them as their parents did. If you find yourself frequently drawn into relationships with narcissistic people, you must figure out what the attraction is for you, see past fantasy to reality, find the courage to set limits and the clarity to recognize your own and others' boundaries, and work at cultivating and maintaining reciprocal relationships. These are your best defenses against the unhealthy narcissism of others, and this book is designed to show you how to apply these principles in your daily life.

Narcissists see themselves as "special people," so Part IV is devoted to exploring in greater depth those particular situations in which narcissism can be especially troubling. With adolescents and in love relationships, for example, there is a fine line between what's normal and what isn't. Narcissists are also more prone to addictive and compulsive behavior because of their special sensitivity to shame. Coping with narcissism on the job or with an elderly parent requires an ability to detach emotionally while still engaging in necessary tasks with equanimity, respect, and compassion. I hope that some of the techniques discussed will help you make better decisions about your own relationships and live with greater peace of mind.

Finally, Part V looks to the future and what needs to be done to get control of the unhealthy narcissism that surrounds us. Our culture is full of narcissistic influences that numb us to the reality of the problems we face. To fight back, we need strong, real Selves that are capable of transcending mere self-interest. When we understand where self-esteem really comes from and make a commitment to raising healthy children—when this becomes our number-one priority—we will have turned the corner toward a better world.

PART I

The Seven Deadly Sins of Narcissism

1

Shamelessness

Stephanie felt the ball leave her racquet cleanly and watched it sail deep into the back court, just inside the baseline. The focus of her attention was split between the path of the ball and her own body mechanics. "Watch the ball," she told herself, "get sideways, hit through, finish up." Forehand after forehand, she repeated her silent mantra until the rhythm of the drill overtook her conscious efforts at control. For a few precious moments, she was in that "zone" that athletes cherish when everything comes together and there are no mistakes.

She was smiling secretly, enjoying a licit high, wondering if her husband, Doug, had also noticed how well she was hitting today, when a heavily underspun return angled into her backhand. She lunged, stabbed, and caught the ball on her racquet rim, sending it flying out of the court. "You never read that spin," Doug scolded from the far court. "Never," Stephanie echoed, suddenly feeling as though she had just blown an internal tire. Pain washed over her and settled in the middle of her chest. She felt too heavy to move her feet, too awkward to connect the racquet at the end of her arm with the small neon projectile hurtling toward her. "I'll never be any good at this game," she thought miserably, smashing the next three balls into the net. The elation of only moments before had evaporated, replaced by a hopeless feeling of ineptitude. Stephanie swallowed the tears rising in her throat and gave herself a mental kick in the backside. "You're such a baby," she muttered to herself as she prepared to pack up and go home. "You wimping out on me again?" Doug called out. He was only teasing, trying to goad her back into the drill, but his words were like salt on a fresh abrasion. There would be no more tennis this day.

Boy, is she touchy, you may be thinking, and you would be right. In my business, we call this a "narcissistic injury," and as trivial as the things that provoke it may seem to an observer, to the injured party, the pain is devastating, as it was for Stephanie in this instance. What seems like a rather mundane occurrence is actually the reopening of a very old wound: a relationship of trust is disrupted by a "misattuned" communication (his criticism colliding with her joy) and, adding insult to injury, Stephanie's trusted husband failed to help make the pain go away. Stephanie's sensitivity, her sudden collapse from a state of pleasure, and her difficulty recovering her emotional balance all point to a very primitive sequence of experiences encoded deep within her psyche, most likely beyond the reach of her conscious memory. It is her hard drive for the emotion of shame.

Shame is among the most unbearable of human feelings, regardless of our age or station in life. Unlike guilt, it speaks not to the misdeed but to the misery of a pervasive personal flaw. We first experience shame in the eyes of our mother or primary attachment figure, when, starting around the age of one, we bring her (usually) our excitement and, instead of sharing our pleasure, she scowls and says, "No!" Her unexpected disapproval shatters the illusion of power and importance that is how we see ourselves at that early age, derived from our union with her. Without warning, we have been ejected from this paradise, and it can only be because we are bad. We feel bad, therefore we are bad.

For some children, this experience, repeated over and over in the course of socialization, is so crushing that they never quite get over it, and they spend their lives avoiding anything that makes them feel ashamed. Recent research in neurobiology has shown that the developing brain is not yet ready to process the intense experience of shame at the age when socialization begins and that the lack of an emotionally attuned parent at this crucial time can actually stunt—for life—the growth of the pathways for regulating such profoundly unpleasant emotions. What helps the infant's brain develop properly is for parents to provide what the young brain is not yet able to, the soothing of the very shame they have inflicted.

Catherine is the mother of a vivacious two-year-old who is the apple of her family's eye. When Janey had to share her mother's attention with a visiting infant one day, she expressed her indignation by hitting the baby. Catherine was horrified and scolded her daughter, then sent her to her room in tears of shame. Catherine felt compassion for her daughter, however, and did not let her sit with the humiliation too long. After a few moments, she went to her and said, "It was bad to hit the baby, and you must never do that again. But you are a good girl, and Mommy loves you. Now, let's go say 'I'm sorry' to Betsy," and then she gave her a hug. Together, they returned to the living room and Catherine helped Janey apologize.

When parents do not respond as Catherine did to soothe the shame they inflict, children develop their own means of compensating—they wall off the intolerable feeling, and they use fantasy to distance themselves from the monster behind the wall. They cling to notions of themselves as special, powerful, or important.

In the Narcissist, shame is so intolerable that the means have been developed not to experience it at all. What psychologists call "bypassed shame" looks like shamelessness or the absence of a conscience, hiding behind a protective barrier of denial, coldness, blame, or rage. Since there are no healthy internal mechanisms available to process this painful feeling, the shame is directed outward, away from the Self. It can never be "my fault."

I recall one young woman I worked with from her late teens until her mid-twenties. A child of divorce who had been alternately pampered and ignored by her self-centered father, she struggled mightily with chronic feelings of low self-worth. She saw herself as stupid and repeatedly acted out her sense of incompetence. These feelings, however, and the shame that accompanied them, were close to the surface compared with the humiliation she felt at having been rejected and abandoned by her father. The depth of that pain was to be dramatically expressed one day shortly after she learned that he had been diagnosed with cancer. "Just in time for my wedding," she said, her mouth contorting in an ugly sneer. "He's never paid for anything in my life." The specter of his possible death—the ultimate abandonment—had pushed her past the shame of inadequacy to a state of congealed rage. She showed not even a hint of embarrassment at the coldness of her outburst, only raw, wounded contempt.

More typically, the shamelessness of the Narcissist comes across as cool indifference or even amorality. We sense that these people are emotionally shallow, and we may think of them as thick-skinned, sure of themselves, and aloof. Then, all of a sudden, they may surprise us by reacting to some minor incident or social slight. When shaming sneaks past the barriers, these "shameless" ones are unmasked for what they really are—supremely shame-sensitive. That is when you will see a flash of hurt, usually followed by rage and blame. When the stink of shame has penetrated their walls, they fumigate with a vengeance.

Shame is the feeling that lurks beneath all unhealthy narcissism, and the inability to process shame in healthy ways—to face it, neutralize it, and move on as healthier individuals do—leads to the characteristic postures, attitudes, and behavior of the Narcissist.

2

Magical Thinking

THE NEED TO AVOID SHAME at all costs creates a continuing dilemma for the Narcissist, as life has a way of regularly doling out humbling experiences that cannot be taken in stride. There is always someone who is better, brighter, more beautiful, more successful, more anything-you-can-think-of. The fact that no one is perfect is of little comfort to Narcissists, however, because they see themselves as the exception to this natural law. Their challenge is to find a way to stay pumped up inside in order to hold these harsh realities at bay. The methods they typically employ involve a considerable amount of distortion and illusion, what psychologists call "magical thinking."

Consider a woman I will call Celeste, who every December holds a holiday open house that she is convinced is the party of the season. The planning of this event consumes her for months at a time. Well in advance, she becomes obsessed with considerations of what food and drink she will serve, how she will decorate her large and impressive home, who will be on the guest list, and, especially, what she will wear. It is important that she find a gown fit for a diva, because the evening's featured entertainment is always Celeste's now traditional rendering of "O Holy Night!," accompanied by her son on the piano.

Celeste fancies herself someone who, had she not been swept off her feet by the dashing young attorney who became her husband, would have spent her life taking curtain calls in the magnificent opera houses of the world. Although he wooed her away from her calling, as she is fond of saying, she still has "the gift" and must share it with the cultured audience of "close friends and admirers" who are annually summoned to this command performance. The truth is, her guests numb themselves at her bar in order to survive the ordeal. Celeste, however, is unaware of their discomfort or, for that matter, that scarcely a one of these "close friends and admirers" considers her more than an eccentric acquaintance. On this evening and for all the hours spent in preparation and fantasy, no reality intrudes.

Celeste has come to depend on her fantasies to insulate herself from an inner emptiness. She sees her world in a romanticized way, with herself and her loved ones in idealized roles. In her mind, her talent is exceptional, her husband and son are storybook heroes, her "friends" are practically royalty, and her life is a never-ending fairy tale. The stories she tells herself allow her to feel special and in control, and anything that might shatter her illusions is simply ignored or dismissed. Family and acquaintances alike learn to handle this denial of reality with kid gloves, because any serious rupture in the bubble she has created threatens to expose the shame of her self-deception and release an underlying rage.

Not all of those who depend on idealization require themselves to be the centerpiece of the fantasy, however. Some, in fact, abhor the limelight and prefer to "bask in the glow" of another's luminescence. These so-called closet Narcissists maintain their grandiosity and omnipotence through a connection to someone *they* can pump up. They are masters of the art of flattery and make the most devoted lovers or friends—up until the time when, for whatever reason, they can no longer sustain the illusion of their chosen one's specialness. Then, sometimes without the slightest warning, their admiration simply dissolves, and they move on to some new object of worship. You will know you have been involved with one of these types when you feel like Cinderella after the clock strikes midnight, sitting there in rags with the pumpkin and the mice. In retrospect, you may realize that the way this person made you feel when things were good was also a little unreal. But when your jokes have never been so funny nor your thoughts so scintillating, when someone's face lights up every time you enter the room, it can be pretty irresistible.

The fantasy world of Narcissists can have a seductive allure that promises to envelop you in its specialness. Their superficial charm can be enchanting, and they often appear complicated, colorful, and exciting as they draw you into their narcissistic web. Being singled out for attention can be an intoxicating sensation in any case, but when the admirer is a Narcissist, that lovely feeling often ends abruptly and unexpectedly. When you cease to be of use in pumping up this person's fragile ego, you, too, may feel that the air has suddenly been let out of your own ego. This can be devastating, especially if it happens repeatedly in a significant relationship, such as one with a family member or a boss. It is not uncommon, in the presence of such individuals, to feel controlled, manipulated, helpless, and angry—or on an emotional rollercoaster ride. Narcissists exude a powerful force field that is difficult to stay clear of and nearly impossible to control once you have been drawn in. They play on whatever narcissistic vulnerabilities you may have left over from earlier experiences with similar characters.

In addition to magical thinking, there are other, more hurtful ways that Narcissists distort reality. The most toxic of these is a process whereby they transfer to someone else whatever evokes shameful feelings in themselves. What psychologists call "projection," I have renamed shame-dumping, a common phenomenon in narcissistic families. A mother who is conflicted about her own sexual desires, for example, may call her teenaged daughter a slut and even succeed in getting the young woman to accept that label and begin behaving promiscuously. It is as if the daughter is a blank screen onto which the mother has projected her unacceptable lust. While it is effective in protecting the narcissistic parent from feeling shame, it is deadly for the child. Children who grow up in such toxic environments frequently suffer from low self-esteem when a parent's shame projections become part of their identity.

Magical thinking, exploitive idealization, and the devaluation of others via shame-dumping and belittling are all attempts on the part of the Narcissist to avoid feeling defective and insignificant. At best, these tactics create barriers to intimacy and acceptance. In a relationship with such a character, you will never know what it is like to be loved and appreciated for who you really are. At worst, the unending distortions will confuse you and wear away your self-esteem.

3

Arrogance

THE PERSONA THAT MANY NARCISSISTS present to the world often comes across to others as a "superiority complex." But behind the mask of arrogance is a fragile internal balloon of self-esteem that is never satisfied with being good or even very good—if they are not *better than,* then they are worthless. Value is always relative, never absolute. From their point of view, if someone else's stock goes up, theirs automatically goes down. Conversely, if they are feeling deflated, they can reinflate themselves by diminishing, debasing, or degrading someone else. This is the reason why Narcissists are often bossy, judgmental, perfectionistic, and power-hungry. They are simply trying to secure the kind of status that will afford them the most distance from the taint of personal defect and shame. If their balloon gets torn by the ill winds of life, they can repair themselves by showing someone else to be inferior. At times, this can be very subtle.

Francine came to see me when she had been having panic attacks for nearly a month. Consciously, her anxiety centered on her husband's recent slide into depression and the specific fear that he might lose his job. Although she spoke of the intense sexual connection that had sustained their troubled marriage for a decade, it was clear that his current emotional crisis had caused her to devalue him. In fact, she said, she was giving serious consideration to divorce. Distancing from him and the failure he represented seemed like the only way to restore her own equilibrium.

Francine needed me to know that she was well-educated, artistically gifted, and had risen above an assortment of personal misfortunes that had shaped her life. There had been a previous failed marriage, a drug habit, a bankruptcy, and, most notably, a depression of her own that had resulted from a work situation in which she had felt disrespected and out of control. She related these stories with a kind of aloofness, communicating a sense that she was not really responsible for any of her problems, an emotional detachment that is characteristic of the way narcissistic individuals bypass shame. There was neither pain nor embarrassment in the telling, but rather a sense that it was remarkable that so many bad things could have happened to someone such as her. In her eyes, she was a noble victim who had triumphed over adversity.

Although her health insurance limited our work to a type of short-term treatment called "solution-focused" therapy, Francine resisted my efforts to provide structure and help her set behavioral goals that could be accomplished in six to twelve sessions. When I attempted to interpret her predicament, she was quick to let me know if I was at all imprecise. I soon learned that my job was simply to reflect back the wonder of her unique strength, and with as few words as possible. To have allowed me to be any more helpful than that would have meant that I was in the superior position in our relationship, which was not at all acceptable. At times, I felt rather superfluous, as if I had little of value to contribute to her recovery. But that was exactly how Francine needed me to feel, and the subtle diminishment of me was to be part of her healing.

As I bore witness, neither challenging nor intruding but accepting her need to feel superior at my expense, Francine shifted her attention from her husband's shortcomings to restoring her injured self-image. She became preoccupied with the intricacies of her own body, which was nearly as sensitive to food and medication as that of the princess in the fairy tale who could feel a pea through a mountain of mattresses. She began to nurture herself and grow more confident, confident enough, in fact, to compete for and win a plum job that would take her career in a new direction. My willingness to tolerate her subtle putdowns may have spared her husband from being similarly used and bought him some time for his own recovery. In any event, the marriage survived that particular crisis, and Francine's panic attacks also subsided. But it was being selected out of a pool of competitors for the job of her dreams that really put Francine back on top.

For Narcissists, competition of all kinds is a way to reaffirm superiority, although many will only compete when they anticipate a favorable outcome. Deeply shamed by defeat, they tend to choose arenas in which they can shine without much risk or effort, and when success happens, they may become compulsive in their pursuit of perfection. Along the way, they crave admiration from others. Admiration-seeking among such Narcissists usually means they are feeling a little unsure of their own superiority and in need of some refueling.

Those who are less successful at developing a talent or skill may rely on petty games of oneupmanship to sustain a sense of superiority. These are among the name-droppers, status seekers, and know-it-alls of the world who may not be able to depend on their accomplishments to prove that they are better than you. "Sore losers" are often Narcissists who cannot bear to be exposed as less than the best. For them, there is nothing acceptable about being ordinary or average—if they can't be superior, they are nothing.

Narcissists are seldom able to sustain a sense of superiority on their own and so are drawn to the limelight and the praise, applause, and recognition from others that keep them inflated. They can be quite sensitive to others' opinions and often have unrealistic expectations of unconditional approval and admiration, even when their actual performance would not merit such a response.

If having an appreciative audience is good, having control over them is even better. Power for the Narcissist is not only an affirmation of superiority but also a means of controlling others to ensure "narcissistic supplies"—anything that feeds a fragile ego. The more power they have, the more freely they can diminish others to keep themselves inflated. This misuse of power in the service of someone's narcissism has become an all-too-familiar feature of many modern work environments, causing morale and performance problems on the job and severe dysfunction within families. At the root of the harm inflicted on others is the need to get rid of the exaggerated shame of real or imagined inferiority.

An arrogant and superior attitude thus serves as a protective barrier that keeps the "stink" of imperfection off the Narcissist, providing insulation from intolerable feelings of shame about personal shortcomings. This person carries within the burning eyes of a critical, shaming parent that must be avoided at any cost. So when you encounter arrogance, it's not really pride that you're seeing, it's a deep and irrational fear of being worthless. The only way to still that fear is to feel important—more important than anyone else, as it turns out.

4

Envy

THE NARCISSIST'S NEED TO SECURE a sense of superiority encounters an obstacle whenever someone else appears to have something that he or she lacks. Pop goes the internal balloon as the other's threat to the superiority of Me registers deep within the unconscious. "Crisis! Crisis!" sounds the alarm. "Better activate the neutralizer!" What weapon does the Narcissist choose to silence the rumblings of shame?

The answer is contempt. "That so-and-so isn't such a big deal as he thinks he is." Never mind that the "so-and-so" may be utterly humble and completely unaware of having given offense—this is a narcissistic distortion akin to shame-dumping and may have no connection to reality. Then comes the laundry list of the other's flaws, and it can get pretty dirty. The intent, usually quite unconscious, is to soil the other enough so that the Narcissist, by comparison, is restored to the superior position. There may be awareness of feelings of disdain (always justified, of course), but the feeling of envy will be adamantly denied. To admit to envy would be to acknowledge inferiority, which no good Narcissist would ever do.

Contempt is usually verbalized but may also be expressed in behavior. I once saw a married couple whose shame-sensitivity was creating serious problems in their relationship. Both were attorneys, and used to calling the shots. For their first session, the husband arrived late, and I detected a faint aroma of alcohol. "I peed in your bushes," he announced as we introduced ourselves. For a moment, I didn't know what to say. Then I realized how excruciating it was for him to explore his marital difficulties with a stranger whose vulnerabilities were allowed to remain hidden. Even before we met, he must have been thinking, "Who is she to sit in judgment of me?" And so he defiled my shrubbery—and made sure I knew what he'd done.

A bright young man named Joel, a graduate student whose family dynamics have left him with narcissistic wounds, explored his problem with envy one day. "There's this guy in my program who just bugs me, and I don't know why," he told me. "He's really pretty nice, but he's married, and, for some reason, that bothers me. I keep thinking he's missing out on going to bars and hitting on women. I mean, we're the same age, and I'm out having fun and he's married. Why should I care if he's married or not? Why should that make me look down on him?"

Joel had grown up with a father who had fallen short of his own ambitions and was very critical of his son. Joel's mother seemed to think of her husband as a failure and clearly wanted her son to do better. There was a great deal of pressure on Joel to achieve, to take the high road at all times, and when he fell short of what eventually became his own expectations, the voice that admonished him from within seemed like his own. But hearing this voice invariably made him angry. The minute his nose left the grindstone, he felt conflicted and defensive. Much of what he considered "fun" was no more than a compulsive quest to vanquish the critical inner parent. The club-hopping and weekend drinking binges and scoring with women who meant nothing to him were all part of a struggle to be just a regular guy, to defy that critical, demanding inner parent.

But when Joel encountered a peer who was happily married and settled down, the bar was raised on what could be expected from a man in his twenties, and Joel didn't measure up. The inner parent began to carp: "Why can't you grow up and be a responsible adult?" But Joel wasn't listening. He was too busy doing damage control. "There's nothing wrong with *me*," his inner defender cried out. "I'm just doing what any red-blooded twenty-four-year-old is supposed to do. It's that married guy who's weird. Imagine that, married at twenty-four!"

Joel at first resisted the idea that what he was experiencing was envy, but when we put the pieces together, it all began to make sense to him. He certainly didn't envy the guy for being married, but he did covet his colleague's appearance of maturity, which made his own weekend revelries seem adolescent by comparison. Envy knows intuitively that the best defense is a good offense, so he began to look down on his colleague.

Sometimes the haughty face of envy is disguised beneath a mask of excessive praise or admiration, often followed by a self-disparaging remark. "This is the *best* cheesecake I've ever eaten! I *so* admire people who can bake. You know, I'm all thumbs in the kitchen. How do you do it and still run your own business? You're just so *talented!*" Your cheesecake has exposed the Narcissist's culinary inadequacy, for which there is no ready defense. So in a grand gesture, she cedes the kitchen to you and relocates her superiority in the moral realm. "I may not be able to bake, but no one could be more appreciative or generous than I. Nice little cheesecake, but I'm still better than you." Watch how quickly the conversation shifts once the Narcissist reconnects to her superiority. There won't be any more talk about your baked goods, or any of your other talents either.

Obsequiousness toward those in power is another version of envy in disguise. Someone else's power is very threatening to a Narcissist and evokes not only envy and contempt but fear of retaliation. Ingratiating behavior helps suppress dangerous thoughts and impulses while at the same time attempting to control the other person. By pleasing the one in power, the Narcissist may even be able to acquire some power of his or her own or "bask in the glow" of connection to someone perceived as superior.

Envy is such a common human foible that it made the biblical list of deadly sins. It is one of the reasons why we are fascinated when the rich, the famous, the brilliant, and the beautiful come to an untimely or ignominious end. "The bigger they are, the harder they fall" is more than a warning against hubris. There is something dark within us that gloats when the grand and glorious are toppled from their pedestals. We love their flaws and misfortunes, because it means that there is not so much distance between us.

Narcissistic envy, fueled by the desperate need to be superior, is something far darker. Like so much else that goes on within the Narcissist, it is unconscious or denied, which makes it that much more dangerous. Unaware of either envy or the need for superiority, these individuals may feel only self-righteous contempt. And that, dear reader, is just another word for hate.

5

Entitlement

SOME TIME AGO, A DISTRAUGHT YOUNG WOMAN came to see me just weeks before her wedding. Her mother wasn't speaking to her, she told me with tears streaming down her cheeks, and it had all begun over a difference of opinion regarding the color of the bridesmaids' gowns. Uncharacteristically, as it turned out, the daughter had refused on this occasion to give in to her mother's wishes and had insisted on the colors of her choice. Mother was enraged. Not only would she not speak to her daughter, but she refused to attend her bridal showers and told anyone who would listen what an ingrate she had turned out to be. My patient was anguished and tried mightily to make amends. She sent small gifts and thanked her mother earnestly for giving her such a beautiful wedding. But Mother would not be moved. She returned the gifts unopened and carried her grudge right into the big day, participating only perfunctorily in the ceremony and leaving the reception early. She even refused copies of the wedding pictures. The bride continued to reach out for reconciliation, but it was months before her mother would even return a phone call. Even after they resumed a tentative relationship, Mother never acknowledged having any part in the estrangement. It was all her daughter's fault.

It is hard to imagine a mother who could be so unyielding as to spoil her loving daughter's wedding day over something as inconsequential as the color scheme. But it is the nature of narcissistic entitlement to see the situation from only one very subjective point of view that says, "My feelings and needs are all that matter, and whatever I want, I should get." Mutuality and reciprocity are entirely alien concepts, because others exist only to agree, obey, flatter, and comfort— in short, to anticipate and meet *my* every need. If you cannot make yourself useful in meeting *my* need, you are of no value and will most likely be treated accordingly, and if you defy *my* will, prepare to feel *my* wrath. Hell hath no fury like the Narcissist denied.

Narcissists hold these unreasonable expectations of particularly favorable treatment and automatic compliance because they consider themselves uniquely special. In social situations, you will talk about them or what they are interested in because they are more important, more knowledgeable, or more captivating than anyone else. Any other subject is boring and won't hold their interest, and, in their eyes, they most certainly have a right to be entertained. In personal relationships, their sense of entitlement means that you must attend to their needs but they are under no obligation to listen to or understand you. If you insist that they do, you are "being difficult" or challenging their rights. How dare you put yourself before me? they seem to (or may actually) ask. And if they have real power over you, they feel entitled to use you as they see fit, and you must not question their authority. Any failure to comply will be considered an attack on their superiority. Defiance of their will is a narcissistic injury that can trigger rage and self-righteous aggression.

The conviction of entitlement is a holdover from the egocentric stage of early childhood, around the age of one to two, when children experience a natural sense of grandiosity that is an essential part of their development. This is a transitional phase, and soon it becomes necessary for them to integrate their feelings of self-importance and invincibility with an awareness of their real place in the overall scheme of things that includes a respect for others. In some cases, however, the bubble of specialness is never popped, and in others the rupture is too harsh or sudden, as when a parent or caretaker shames excessively or fails to offer soothing in the wake of a shaming experience. Whether overwhelmed with shame or artificially protected from it, children whose infantile fantasies are not gradually transformed into a more balanced view of themselves in relation to others never get over the belief that they are the center of the universe. Such children may become self-absorbed "entitlement monsters," socially inept and incapable of the small sacrifices of Self that allow for reciprocity in personal relationships. The undeflated child turns into an arrogant adult who expects others to serve as constant mirrors of his or her wonderfulness. In positions of power, they can be egotistical tyrants who will have their way without regard for anyone else.

Like shame, the rage that follows frustrated entitlement is a primitive emotion that we first learn to manage with the help of attuned parents. The child's normal narcissistic rages, which intensify during the power struggles of age eighteen to thirty months—those "terrible twos"—require "optimal frustration" that is neither overly humiliating nor threatening to the child's emerging sense of Self. When children encounter instead a rageful, contemptuous, or teasing parent during these moments of intense arousal, the image of the parent's face is stored in the developing brain and called up at times of future stress to whip them into an aggressive frenzy. Furthermore, the failure of parental attunement during this crucial phase can interfere with the development of brain functions that inhibit aggressive behavior, leaving children with lifelong difficulties controlling aggressive impulses.

Conversely, under optimal circumstances, children encode a memory of a "quietly available" parent who accepts and contains unruly behavior, helping them to regulate rage and shame as well as to delay reacting. The "good enough" parent can tolerate strong negative feelings in the child and has enough self-control not to lash out in retaliation. In essence, the child takes in the parent's compassionate behavior, and it becomes a part of his or her own sense of worthiness.

It is not worthiness the Narcissist feels when he or she communicates "I deserve." Narcissistic entitlement has nothing to do with genuine self-esteem, which comes from real accomplishment and being true to one's own ideals. Individuals who feel entitled to respect without giving it in return, or who expect rewards without effort, or a life free of discomfort, are forfeiting any power they might have to shape their own destiny. They assume an essentially passive role and count on outside forces to make them happy. When what they expect doesn't happen, they feel impotent. By claiming entitlement, they demand to live in the fantasy world of the one-year-old child. No wonder they're enraged.

Entitlement and the rage that comes with it are tip-offs to the arrest in healthy development that is narcissism.

6

Exploitation

THE ABILITY TO EMPATHIZE, to grasp accurately how another person feels and to feel compassionate in response, requires us to step outside ourselves momentarily to tune in to someone else. We turn down the noise of our own preoccupations and open ourselves to what the other person is expressing. We may or may not share the feelings being expressed, but we accept them without judgment or distortion. Even when we identify with another person's feelings, we remain separate.

Although we do not actually become one with the other person in moments of empathy, we do bridge the gap between two separate beings. That cannot happen unless we are able to experience ourselves as separate in the first place. The sense of one's Self as separate and autonomous is a developmental milestone that normally occurs in small increments between the ages of one to three or four. In order to read others accurately, we must first be able to see ourselves in realistic terms and identify our feelings as belonging to us.

Empathic parenting in the face of a small child's intense feelings helps to form the building blocks of a developing capacity for compassion. Children aged ten to fourteen months have been observed to become agitated and disturbed when they see their mothers are distressed, and this may be the earliest expression of what will one day be empathy. By eighteen months, the emotionally healthy child becomes capable of internally regulating her own distress and able to offer comfort to others. Empathy will not develop, however, unless the child achieves a separate sense of Self and the capacity to tolerate a range of emotions, including shame. Bypassed shame—the shame that narcissistic people so deeply suppress that it remains beneath conscious awareness—stunts the growth of empathy. Without empathy, people have difficulty controlling aggressive impulses.

Driven by shame and prone to rage and aggression, the Narcissist never develops the capacity to identify with or even to recognize the feelings and needs of others. This is a person who, in terms of emotional development, got stuck around the age of one to two. Others are not seen as separate entities but rather as extensions of Self, there to do the Narcissist's bidding. This, along with an underdeveloped conscience, tends to make them interpersonally exploitative.

A young woman—let's call her Melanie—whom I had been treating for depression took months to find the courage to reveal to me a shocking family secret. Her mother, a retired professional woman, had applied for credit cards in Melanie's name and, over an extended period of time, had run up huge bills that she had made no attempt to repay. Melanie, who earned a modest income as a civil servant and could barely afford her own expenses, was struggling to make payments as her mother continued to charge away. I asked her why she tolerated this situation. "Oh, you don't want to make my mother angry!" she replied without hesitation. That, I guess, would have been worse than major credit card debt.

Stealing her credit was only one of the ways that this mother used her daughter mercilessly. She also expected her to become a paying tenant whenever the family's income property was vacant and to help out with her younger sister's college expenses. The lack of concern for or even awareness of Melanie's wishes, needs, and circumstances was truly stunning. By using her without regard for her feelings, Melanie's mother had taught her to think of her own value in very limited ways. Not surprisingly, Melanie only felt worthwhile when she was taking care of others, and she had a great deal of difficulty asserting herself. She needed to attach herself to someone more substantial in order to feel real.

Exploitation can take many forms but always involves the using of others without regard for their feelings or interests. Often the other is in a subservient position where resistance would be difficult or even impossible. Sometimes the subservience is not so much real as assumed. The offense can be as mild as a one-sided friendship in which one gives and the other takes, as commonplace as a selfish lover or a demanding boss, or as horrendous as sexual predation and harassment on the job. It may or may not involve deceit but quite often includes distortions of reality.

Jesse was one of the top salesmen at a large industrial chemical company. A divorced father in his early forties, he came to see me because his on-again-off-again girlfriend of three years had told him that if he didn't get some professional help, it would be off again for good. Jesse didn't want to lose her. They had a great sex life when she wasn't angry with him, and she could cook all his favorite foods just the way he liked them. Besides, he told me with a little wink, the way she looked in a cocktail dress made the other guys green with envy whenever he took her to company parties.

Jesse wanted to know what I, as a woman, thought he should do to keep his girlfriend from breaking up with him. I asked him what he thought she wanted. "Oh," he said, "she wants some kind of commitment. She'd like it if I moved in with her, showed her I could be a domestic type. She'd like a kid someday—I guess her time is running out. Me, I got two kids. I don't really need that, you know." And what, I asked, did Jesse need? "I just want things to stay like they are, only without her getting so mad all the time. The way she gets on my case is really a drag."

Jesse was in many ways a charming and likeable guy. He was very goal-oriented and energetic, and he knew how to have a good time. There wasn't a mean bone in his body, but neither did he have an ounce of compassion for anyone else. He was about a quarter of an inch deep, and everything was about Me. When others became enraged by his lack of sensitivity, he seldom got angry back. It just puzzled him that anybody could get so upset when all he was trying to do was get ahead or be happy. He displayed many of the hallmarks of narcissism, not the least of which was his interpersonal exploitation and total lack of awareness or conscience about this character flaw.

Jesse decided to distance himself from his girlfriend but couldn't quite break it off as long as she was still willing to sleep with him. Seeing less of her gave him some respite from her anger, but it also made him feel anxious and alone. He hooked up with a couple of old girlfriends and even had sex with his ex-wife, who evidently still had feelings for him. His children suddenly became very important to him, and he boasted to me about how close he had become to his sixteen-year-old daughter. "She's like my best friend," he said proudly. "We can talk about anything." He thought it was probably good for her that he had been intimate with her mother. "She feels like we're a family again." But, of course, this "family feeling" only lasted as long as it met Jesse's needs.

7

Bad Boundaries

WE ARE BY NATURE SOCIAL CREATURES who thrive on meaningful affiliations with family, friends, and community. We all need to "belong" to something, someone outside of ourselves. We are also, however, unique individuals who have private thoughts, personal feelings, and a body that belongs only to ourselves. Although we were not meant to live as islands, completely self-involved and cut off from other people, we are programmed from birth to evolve into separate beings with an autonomous Self. The soundness of the boundary between Self and others will affect not only how we perceive ourselves but how we experience other people and to a considerable extent how we are treated by them. Good boundaries, the recognition of separateness, make for healthy relationships.

The Narcissist suffers from a deep character flaw in the development of a sense of Self. This flaw prevents such individuals from being able to recognize that they have boundaries and that others are separate and not extensions of themselves. Others either exist to meet their needs or may as well not exist at all. Those who offer the possibility of some sort of gratification will be treated as if they are a part of the Narcissist and will be expected, automatically, to live up to that person's expectations. In the mind of a Narcissist, there is no boundary between Self and other.

The reason why Narcissists function this way goes back to their experiences in early childhood. As anyone who has ever spent any time around small children knows, they go through an egocentric stage when they seem to feel very important and invincible. This begins to occur about the same time they start to walk and normally continues into the twos. Their egocentric behavior is usually viewed by adults as anywhere from endearing to exasperating, but it has a very important function. The child in this stage is actually beginning to form the first sense of himself as separate from his primary caregivers, and an inflated sense of self-importance allows him to explore the world without overwhelming fears and doubts.

Before this point, the child has experienced himself psychologically as indistinguishable from the person he is most attached to, the one who has been most responsible for his care. He sees this person as wonderful and powerful and himself as the same because, in his infant mind, they are one. When he begins to get the picture that he is small and helpless, that the power resides in the other person and not himself, a part of him wishes to stay in this fantasy of union with the powerful caregiver. If there are no boundaries between them, he can continue to feel control over the one who meets his needs.

It is one of the jobs of parents to ease the small child through this time of emotional vulnerability by helping her to accept that, while she is separate and relatively powerless, she is valuable for who she really is. If parents allow the child to feel too important or to have too much control, the child maintains her infantile fantasy that her power comes from controlling her powerful parents. This stands in the way of her developing an appreciation of her own real capabilities and the confidence to stand alone. Instead, she hones skills of scanning the environment for others who can give her what she lacks or needs. If she can convince them that she is special, they will admire her and she can share in their power. This is a rather desperate quest, and those who cannot be used will be discarded. Those who are useful, however, are perceived, like the parents, as extensions of the Self and treated as if they had no separate existence.

I recall the story of a patient of mine who came home one day to find that her mother-in-law had replaced her living room furniture. Without consulting my patient, the mother-in-law had selected a beautiful new sofa and matching chairs and arranged to have them delivered, and the old furniture disposed of, as a "surprise." My patient was indeed surprised—and dismayed. True, she had been planning to replace the old furniture, but she had been looking forward to shopping and making her own choices. That she might want to do this never crossed the mother-in-law's mind. Her son and his wife had purchased her old home, so she knew what would look good in the living room, and besides, she felt like giving them a gift. The younger couple also both worked for the mother-in-law, so she was used to having control in their lives. There were many boundary violations in this family.

People who tolerate boundary violations are generally those who, like the Narcissist, have not formed a strong sense of separate Self, usually because they have been trained to accept intrusions while growing up in their own families and have not been given support for autonomy. Others from such backgrounds are very sensitized to these intrusions and erect rigid boundaries to protect themselves. These are the people who have difficulty trusting and allowing intimacy in close relationships. They develop an anxious, apprehensive attitude toward others, as if they expect to be violated in some way. Sometimes, however, their lack of experience with healthy boundaries makes them confused or unsure when an intrusion is occurring. Such was the case with my patient whose mother-in-law replaced her furniture. She knew that she was unhappy about this gift but blamed herself for being unappreciative. Who wouldn't want beautiful new furniture? she reasoned. It took quite a bit of discussion before she was able to understand why she felt so uncomfortable.

The Narcissist is often equally unaware when violating the personal boundaries of others. Mail and personal journals or diaries are read; closed bathroom and bedroom doors are ignored; purses and wallets are rifled through; clothing, toiletries, and other possessions are "borrowed"; conversations are eavesdropped on; nosy questions are asked; unsolicited opinions are offered; ideas are stolen; confidences are not kept; hugs and kisses and other kinds of touch are forced on someone whose resistance is overlooked. Many of my patients report being told, "That's not how you feel," or, "This is what you think," or even, "This is who you are." When confronted with these violations, the Narcissist is often annoyed or even mystified. In a world without fences, why should they have to knock on doors?

When many or most of the Seven Deadly Sins are present in an individual who presents for mental health services, that person may be diagnosed with a Narcissistic Personality Disorder, a relatively rare condition. The American Psychiatric Association estimates that only about one in one hundred people meets the full criteria for this severe form of narcissism, yet there are many more individuals who exhibit these traits to some degree sufficient to cause significant distress, if not in themselves, then certainly in others with whom they come in close contact on a regular basis. Many of these individuals never come to the attention of mental health professionals because they are too shame-intolerant to recognize their own narcissism and are more inclined to blame others when they are in pain. Even when they seek help, they are more likely to be treated for depression, anxiety, relationship difficulties, or job-related stress than for the Narcissistic Personality Disorder that lies beneath their presenting problems. Many therapists miss or ignore the narcissism because it is not amenable to the short-term approaches currently favored by the insurance companies who pay for treatment. Sadly, treatment is often not effective in these cases, because the more narcissistic people are, the more rigid and resistant they are to behavioral change.

While a narcissistic personality that meets the full criteria for a clinical diagnosis may be relatively rare—and we should all avoid labels that trigger shame in others—there is plenty of evidence that toxic levels of narcissism are pandemic in American society and have been for some time (see Chapter 19 for a discussion of this). You are likely to recognize the Seven Deadly Sins in many people you encounter, and perhaps even in yourself. This book is designed to help you make sense of these experiences and to better protect yourself from being used in ways that undermine your healthy self-esteem. Don't be surprised, however, if along the way you have to own up to some unhealthy narcissism of your own. This is to be expected if you were raised in a family where one or both parents were significantly narcissistic, leaving you vulnerable in many ways. You may share with the more flagrant Narcissist an impaired sense of interpersonal boundaries, considerable shame-sensitivity, a tendency to distort reality, and more anger than you can account for. You may feel drawn to narcissistic characters and also be more reactive to them than others are. Your strength, however, is in having enough shame tolerance to be able to learn about this problem and make changes that will improve the quality of your life. Starting with Part III, you will find out how.

But first, it is important to understand how a Narcissist comes to be, so that you know exactly what (or whom) you are up against. As you shall see, we all go through a stage of normal narcissism in early childhood, and the way we are parented determines how much of that we carry forward—and in what ways.

PART II

Where Does Narcissism Come From?

8

Childhood Narcissism
and the Birth of "Me"

EVERY CHILD IS BORN WITH the psychological hardwiring to become a Narcissist. In fact, this is one of the things that make the "terrible twos" (and sometimes the threes) so terrible, as all children go through a stage when grandiosity and omnipotence are normal ways of thinking, and the sense of entitlement that goes with these attitudes can trigger rage when an infantile will is thwarted. Shame is not in the emotional repertoire at the beginning of this stage, but it will become a major force for the child to contend with before completing early emotional development. How well children learn to manage shame is what will ultimately determine who becomes a Narcissist. It all begins with the task of forming a healthy sense of Self as distinct from one's caregivers, what psychologists call "the process of separation-individuation." This concept refers to the establishment of boundaries between Self and Other, the ability to distinguish what is Me and what is You. As we saw in the last chapter, the Narcissist lacks such clear boundaries, but in fact, we all started out that way.

Primary and Secondary Narcissism

It was nearly a century ago when Sigmund Freud described the infant's initial "autoerotic" (self-loving) state as one of "primary narcissism," by which he meant that all of the baby's "libido," or life force, was focused on itself and its own needs. In the earliest days of life, he theorized, a "stimulus barrier," or natural psychological shield, guarded the infant's immature nervous system against sensory overload from outside. Within its own protective cocoon, he considered the infant an emotionally self-contained being not yet able to conceive of a Self, or of others either, for that matter.

We no longer think of children in this way, thanks to infant research that has shown us how very much newborns are aware and capable of. We now know that even very young babies want stimulation within tolerable limits and can formulate and test simple hypotheses about their "interpersonal world" right from the beginning. Nevertheless, Freud's ideas about narcissism, as elaborated and amended by those who followed him, still form the basis of our understanding of a child's *psychological* development, the birth of Self in earliest childhood.

Freud postulated that when babies began to cry more around the age of two months, it meant that the stimulus barrier was breaking down and the outside world was flooding in in unpleasant ways. He pictured a frantic infant who no longer had the luxury of oblivious self-containment and was forced by this circumstance to recognize that soothing came from outside its own cocoon. The infant's concept of Other was no more developed than its sense of Self, however, and the comforting breast, arms, face, and voice of the primary caretaker became, from this "narcissistic" perspective, part of a rudimentary Me that he likened to a bird's egg composed of two yolks within the same shell.

Freud considered this awakening to the caretaking aspects of another being a progression from the initial state of auroerotism to the earliest form of love for others, with the child still "the center and core" of his own universe. This normal form of "primary" narcissism was thought to last through the first year of life, followed by a period of "secondary narcissism" in which fantasies of his own omnipotence were linked to his inflated perception of his parents, particularly his primary caretaker. By seeing himself as one with his powerful parents, the child could carry a certain sense of invincibility with him as he began to explore his environment.

Think for a moment of the one-year-old child who has just learned to walk and toddles off in all directions in search of adventure. The world is full of dangers, but the securely attached child has no fear at this stage. She is full of a robust quest for discovery and scarcely seems to notice that she is so small and everything around her is big and potentially menacing. I once observed a wobbly youngster who escaped her mother just long enough to step out onto an empty dance floor before a sizable crowd awaiting an awards ceremony. With all eyes on her, she looked around at the assembled mass of smiling faces and began to gyrate along with the music while obviously enjoying the crowd's delight. Standing on the sidelines, her somewhat abashed mother hardly knew what to do, and it took some coaxing to persuade the little actress to cede the floor to the pending ceremony. A star is born? Maybe, but this sort of exaggerated confidence is normal in early childhood and signals that the child carries within her an inflated sense of Self that is linked to an equally inflated sense of her primary caretaker—even when that person is temporarily out of sight. If this looks like a junior version of the older Narcissist's magical thinking, that's because it is. But in toddlerhood, secondary narcissism is still a normal transitional stage that the healthy child relinquishes when she becomes better equipped psychologically to give it up. What prepares a child to let go of this narcissistic position is the gradual development of real competencies that do not depend on inflated fantasies to sustain a sense of efficacy and self-esteem.

The Birth of "Me"

The basic kit that we come equipped with at birth includes many things, but not what psychologists call a "Self." There is, of course, sensation, of hunger and cold, of pain and comfort. And there is perception, too, of light and noise, and most especially, of smell. There is also instinct to root for food, and impulse to cry out when in distress. Each of us is born with a unique genetic endowment, and something called temperament, but the sum of these raw materials we bring from the womb does not yet constitute Self. This must await a second, psychological birth of what each individual will come to think of as "Me."

Like the body and like the mind, the Self unfolds in sequential fashion. It begins with a look from someone who loves us, a gaze so compelling and utterly essential to our very survival that we are convinced the face it emanates from is somehow part of us. The first rudimentary Me resembles that bird's egg of Freud's and includes a particular Other on whom we depend for everything that matters. She (usually) is so important, so powerful, that it will take many months before we fully realize that she is Not Me after all but rather someone quite separate. In the meantime, we take strength from her strength.

Around the age of two to four months, the infant becomes more capable of recognizing a particular caregiver as the one who feeds, soothes, and comforts. A "preferential" smile reserved just for this person appears, and this is thought to be the beginning of a psychological state known as "symbiosis," an important concept in our understanding of how narcissism develops. Symbiosis means that the infant's sense of Self is merged with the caregiving Other—let's call her Mother—and the rest of the world remains pretty much unimportant. Mother and child are in their own private paradise.

A few months later, however, our infant starts to hatch from this symbiotic egg and begins to inspect other people and notice that they are different from Mother. If held by someone else, he will gravely study and possibly try to grab hold of eyes, hair, nose, mouth, glasses, or jewelry, glancing at Mother if she is in sight, making rudimentary comparisons. He has grasped the concept of otherness; now he just has to figure out that Mother is one of them instead of part of Me. That will come later.

By seven to ten months of age, our little guy becomes able to move away from Mother, to crawl, to climb, and to pull himself upright while using her for support. She is still the apple of his eye, but that eye has begun to rove toward the whole big world that's waiting to be explored. Independent mobility gives him the physical distance from which to contemplate Mother as a separate entity, but psychologically, she is now an extension of him and not yet a whole and separate person in his mind.

He carries this "fused" sense of Self with him as he begins to walk at about ten to twelve months of age, and a period of great exuberance ensues that lasts through age sixteen to eighteen months. During this time, bumps, falls, and other frustrations seem to roll right off our sturdy little explorer, and as his adventures take him farther away from Mother, he becomes so absorbed that at times he seems to forget she is there. Then all of a sudden it is as if he runs out of his own steam, and he returns to her for what has been described as "refueling." If he can't find her in these moments, his whole demeanor changes—he may slow down, lose interest in his surroundings, and appear almost somber. Analytic observers describe this as the child turning inward, as if trying to find an image of Mother within himself. If someone else offers to stand in for her at this age, the child may burst into tears of protest. Only after "reunion" with her does he enthusiastically resume his happy explorations. She's still The One, and still very necessary to his sense of confidence.

The child at the beginning of this period (aptly named "practicing") is starting to walk but is not yet able to manage feelings independently. Mother's presence, along with the psychological merger with her that still characterizes his inner life, allows him to cope with both the intense joy and excitement of discovery and the frustrations of being a small and vulnerable person in an expanding world. After periods of separation, her empathic response to his mood will have a far-reaching impact on his developing brain.

Brain research on infants has shown that, during two critical periods, the first between ten and twelve months and the second between sixteen and eighteen months (both ends of the "practicing" phase), the part of the brain that regulates emotions is being hardwired for life. One of the things the child is "practicing," in fact, is how to manage his own feelings, an ability that is essential to a separate sense of Self, an autonomous Me. The sensitive mother is tuned in to her child's moods and helps tone down an overly excited or distressed toddler, but she also knows when to permit that extra bit of tension that allows him to develop his own emotional tolerance.

The child's relationship with the mother shifts noticeably over the course of the practicing phase from approximately ten to eighteen months. If Mother has shown enough pleasure and interest during the symbiotic phase, the child approaches the prospect of moving away from her with high excitement. Around ten months of age, he spends more time awake and more awake time in play, as much as six hours a day. At first, Mother is more like a combination playmate and nursemaid, but over the next six months, she will become the "no-no" person, the one who introduces the cold-shower experience of socialization with her "prohibitive behavior." The intense states of elation so characteristic of the child earlier in this phase begin to shift to "low arousal states" that look like a toddler version of somberness or even mild depression. This "low-keyedness," however, is normal and has an important function—it helps further the growth of a part of the brain that governs energy conservation and the inhibition of emotion. By moving in and out of these low arousal states, the child is learning to tone down intense or unpleasant feelings with less assistance from the outside. Each new skill allows him to be more self-reliant and takes him a step closer to psychological autonomy.

In preparing children to live in harmony with the world of others, socialization aims to restrain undesirable behavior, including many acts they thoroughly enjoy. To persuade a child to give up these pleasures, it is necessary to invoke the powerful emotion of shame. For the child, the first experience of shame is a betrayal of the illusion of perfect union with Mother that has persisted up to this point. Her beloved face now may radiate shame, extinguishing joy and exuberance in an instant. Instead of being pumped up by Mother, the child now feels deflated, even injured. This is an essential and instructive wound, however, which teaches the child that Mother is not only separate but different, and that his place in the world will not always be on top of the mountain. But it is a wound that must be inflicted gently.

Shame is a heavy burden for the one-year-old child, and he must depend on a sensitive, responsive, and emotionally approachable caregiver to soothe him. What is required are soft looks, warm touches, and kind words, initiated by Mother or other caretakers. The experience of elation, shame, and recovery then becomes a positive exercise in learning to manage shame, and another stepping-stone in the development of a healthy sense of Self. The child has learned that hurt feelings can be mended, that he is effective, and that his caregiver can be trusted. When this does not occur, the child perceives instead that his needs and feelings are shameful and unacceptable, and that he is bad. Emotionally, the young child needs compassionate help in managing emotions and protection from overwhelming feelings until his brain matures sufficiently for him to do this on his own.

On the plus side, shame inhibits the natural egotism that comes to full blossom in the practicing stage, and it allows children to become more adept at interacting with others. They need to learn that they are unique and important, but no more unique and important than anyone else, especially their parents. Without humiliating or overwhelming them, caregivers must help children to evolve from a sense of grandiosity and omnipotence that comes from seeing themselves as fused with a wonderful and powerful Mother to a separate sense of Self that is more reality-based. Small doses of shame, followed by soothing, help children transform their grandiosity into a more realistic self-image. Parents and caregivers must be able to tolerate inducing this kind of stress, however, in order for children to develop emotionally. Sometimes that's as hard for parents as it is for the child.

By the end of the practicing period, around the age of eighteen months, the child and the mother can no longer function effectively as a symbiotic Us. The illusion of Mother's omnipotence gradually gives way to the child's recognition that they are different and that she is interested in other people and activities apart from him. The delusions of grandeur that enabled him to explore the world so confidently begin to crash, creating a state of emotional disequilibrium. Until approximately age three, the once-exuberant child is clearly more aware of his real vulnerability and becomes preoccupied with Mother's whereabouts and anxious if she leaves. When she is present, he demands that she share everything with him, hence the name "rapprochement" (French for closeness, or re-establishment of good relations) that has been given to this final phase in the separation-individuation process.

The rapprochement child of eighteen to thirty-six months has more actual capability than the younger toddler but is much more fearful precisely because he can no longer sustain the illusion of his own omnipotence and grandiosity, nor of his mother's fusion with him. His moods and behavior are marked with ambivalence as he alternately approaches Mother to share his world and recapture the joys of symbiosis, then pulls away angrily to assert independence. The rages and tantrums of this age express the child's outrage at both his own growing awareness of his real place in the relative scheme of things and the loss of control over the powerful, benevolent Mother who was once as much a part of him as his own face and hands.

At the end of this challenging phase of dramatic clinging and opposition, the healthy child emerges with a realistic sense of Self and an appreciation for the autonomy of others, which is normally well in place before the age of four. Individuation has occurred, and the child may now be considered to have a whole and separate sense of Me.

Here is how one empathic mother handled some of the challenges of the rapprochement stage:

Emily: A Calm Place to Grow

Twenty-seven-month-old Emily awoke from her afternoon nap to find a stranger in the house. While she had been sleeping, Mother had been entertaining a friend for lunch, and she could hear an unfamiliar voice in the next room on the other side of her closed door. She called out from her bed, and Mother responded immediately. "We have company," Mother told Emily softly, aware that her daughter was not yet fully awake. "Do you want to come meet Sylvie?"

A few minutes of private reconnection ensued before the pair emerged from the bedroom, Emily wrapped tightly around her mother's torso with her blond curls buried in Mother's neck. "She likes to be naked," Mother commented casually to the guest, by way of explaining her daughter's unclad state. Still entwined, the two sat down at the table, and Mother resumed her adult conversation while stroking Emily gently.

Before long, Emily turned around and inspected the stranger warily. Mother acknowledged her joining the group and offered her some food and a drink. The conversation shifted to include Emily, who slowly began to participate by directing comments toward her mother. From time to time, she reached into her mother's shirt to tug on her breast. "We've just been through weaning," Mother explained to the guest, sometimes ignoring her child's grasping hand and at other times simply removing it and redirecting Emily's attention elsewhere. There was no annoyance in Mother's response, nor was there an attempt to shame her daughter. None of those "You're a big girl now" messages.

Emily was by this time fully awake and relaxed in the stranger's presence, but she was clearly not happy to share her mother's attention. "No more talking," she said to the two women, who interrupted their conversation to acknowledge her, then resumed chatting while trying to include her. But inclusion was not what she wanted. "No more talking," Emily repeated. She was not obeyed.

So she began to play with her food and swallow cherry pits in furtive defiance of her mother's warning not to. "It's not okay to throw food on the floor," Mother reminded Emily quietly, again without anger or shaming. "Don't swallow the cherry pits, Emily. You know why? You might choke." And Mother continued to chat with her guest while holding Emily in her lap, interacting with her physically and verbally. Emily stopped playing with her food and began spitting out the cherry pits. "Come on, girlfriend," Mother said to Emily. "Want to show Sylvie your room?"

Indeed, she did, as well as pictures of Daddy, who was much the topic of conversation. In her room, Emily showed the guest more pictures, toys, and, with obvious delight, the reflection of herself in the mirror. Then, for an encore, she sat down on her potty chair and peed. "Oh, good," Mother responded in a tone that exactly matched her daughter's quiet sense of accomplishment. "Do you want to pour it in the toilet?" And she did, and flushed it, too. "That's so good, Emily," Mother said matter-of-factly.

What is impressive about this mother's parenting style is her easy acceptance of exactly where her child is developmentally and her ability to move seamlessly from nurturing and comforting to gentle socialization and then to playfulness and back. Infancy is more over than not for this two-year-old girl, but she is not yet fully ready to let go of the pleasures of being a baby. Notice her possessiveness of her mother's body, her somber assessment of and slowness to warm to the stranger, and how intently she focuses on control of herself and her environment. Notice also how her mother's consistently attuned responses defuse power struggles and respect Emily's emerging autonomy without overplaying or underplaying the socialization card. And look at the results! Emily is well on her way to a healthy and separate sense of Self.

The first two to three years of life are the age of narcissism when the child's underdeveloped Self and lack of awareness of the otherness of others are normal. Grandiosity, omnipotence, magical thinking, shame-sensitivity, and a lack of interpersonal boundaries come with the package. We are meant to outgrow this stage, but we need the help of parents who can tolerate and love us while we get through to the other side. We need them to hold the boundaries that we don't yet see, to recognize who we really are and can be, to help us manage shame and contain rage, and to teach us to live in a world of others. When that doesn't happen, we can become stuck in childhood narcissism. Failure to complete the separation-individuation process is what leads to a narcissistic personality.

In the next chapter, we will look at a particular kind of parent who is unable to assist the child through this passage. When the parent suffers from significant narcissism, the results are predictable. Some children will themselves become clones of their narcissistic parents, while others will be mysteriously drawn into relationships that require a familiar sacrifice of Self.

9

The Narcissistic Parent

WHEN YOU THINK ABOUT IT, steering a child through the narcissistic reefs of the separation-individuation process is one tough job. Optimally, you have to look beyond the egocentrism, the mood swings, the temper tantrums, and the defiance to the person who is struggling with a very important developmental task, the formation of a healthy, autonomous Self. The job requires an adult who is patient, compassionate, and clear on boundaries. To do the job well, parents and caregivers need to have a realistic sense both of themselves and of the child, to be able to control their own aggressive impulses, and, most of all, to *not* use the child to meet their own needs. In short, they must have successfully completed their own separation-individuation process. But what if they haven't?

The Narcissistic Mother

Given that the overture of life is widely heard to be a duet between mother and child—with the father in a significant but nevertheless supporting role—the professional literature has devoted far more attention to narcissistic mothers of young children than to their fathers. Among experts who believe that most of a child's later problems stem from mishaps during the years when a separate Self is being formed, the mother is seen as the one who wields the most power and therefore has the most responsibility. But the crucial person in these formative years, the one who will have the most impact on early psychological development, is really the preferred caretaker with whom the child forms a symbiotic attachment. In today's world, that person might alternatively be a father, a same-sex partner of the biological or adoptive parent, another relative such as a grandparent, a nanny, or someone at the daycare center who tends to a very young child for most of its waking hours. Mothers cannot claim this role by title alone.

That said, it is important to note that when the caretaking mother is a Narcissist, the very process of symbiosis is threatened because of a failure to bond in the normal way. This is a mother who is incapable of forming a healthy attachment to her child, even when she desperately wants to. She can't help but be drawn to motherhood for narcissistic reasons—an idealized vision of herself as a nurturer, perhaps, or a desire to "complete" herself by carrying in her body, bearing, and suckling a child. Images of herself in this archetypal female role ignite her grandiosity and magnify her feelings of entitlement. Even before conception, the fantasized child is an extension of her, someone who can be used to make her feel special and inspire others to admire her.

The narcissistic mother requires, of course, a "perfect" child to mirror *her* perfection as a giver and nurturer of life. If the real child disappoints in some way—by appearance, or sex, or some other flaw—she herself will feel defective, triggering shame and rage. But by projecting another, more pleasing image onto her child, one that promises to pump her up, she can hide her ugly feelings and preserve the admiration of others. Whether she perceives her child as "perfect" or is secretly disappointed, the narcissistic mother does not bond so much with the real infant as with the fantasy child of her dreams.

Signs of a mother's narcissism are evident before the child is born in women who may be excessively preoccupied with their own appearance and comfort during pregnancy, who expect others to cater to them, who are unusually distressed with the changes in their bodies, or who are extremely fearful of labor and delivery. Some may be obsessed with having the perfect pregnancy or becoming a perfect mother. In other cases, a narcissistic mother-to-be may be too absorbed in her own life to seek adequate prenatal care or may engage in practices or activities, such as drug or alcohol use or other risky behavior, that endanger the fetus. She may show little interest in preparing for the arrival of her child, or conversely, she may be obsessed with having "the best of everything," regardless of her financial circumstances. She may have excessive expectations in regard to gifts from relatives and friends or be more interested in decorating the nursery or assembling the layette than in actually welcoming a child into her life. The narcissistic mother-to-be may be either detached from or overly invested in aspects of her pregnancy, but in either case, she is preoccupied with her own experience rather than focused on the infant who will soon emerge from her body.

After her child arrives, the narcissistic mother may become depressed as the crushing demands of a newborn leave little opportunity for her to satisfy her grandiose fantasies. The selflessness required of her at this stage of motherhood may be more than she can bear, and she may look for ways out. She may not hesitate to take advantage of someone else's offer to shoulder some or all of the burden, and if she had a career or a job that she enjoyed, she may be desperate to return sooner than she had originally planned. If there is no way to escape, she may go through the motions with indifference or carelessness, unless others are watching. In these difficult early months when the child has little to offer her that feeds her narcissism, she may be neglectful, overly anxious, or very emotionally detached and mechanical, as if the baby were a doll. Her experience of motherhood may be reflected in comments that attribute unrealistic meanings to her baby's behavior, such as, "He just cries like that to make me mad!"

By the time, a few months later, when their babies are ready to engage in a symbiotic relationship, some narcissistic mothers have already found someone else to take over as primary caregiver. Those who have hung in, however, may be pleased by what is about to happen. Rewarded for their efforts by "the preferential smile," they get to feel special again, at least for a while. Since the narcissistic mother does not recognize boundaries between herself and others anyway and actually prefers to have them mesh with her, she's a natural for the symbiotic phase. Her baby will gaze at her lovingly, study her every move and expression, take comfort only from her touch and her voice, and she will respond in kind. No one, perhaps, has ever made her feel so important, so special. No one has ever belonged to her so completely, not since . . . ever so long ago. Deep within her a chord is struck, evoking a time of rapture from her own infancy. She may become so absorbed in this child who is now psychologically merged with her that she may be unable to attend to anyone else during this time.

Alas, however, her child will soon betray their blissful union. He is destined to outgrow it, to seek his fortunes in the world beyond their private paradise. As she watches him begin to respond to others and pay attention to things that are of little interest to her, she may become resentful or fearful of losing him. She may try to restrict his opportunities for autonomy or control him through excessive shaming. She may also begin to manipulate him by rewarding behavior that resonates with her own selfish expectations, pumping up the child's natural grandiosity during this period and making it difficult for him to develop a more realistic self-concept.

Remember Emily, the two-year-old girl in the last chapter who woke up to find a visitor in her home? Her mother's attuned responses to some of the challenges of the last phase of separation-individuation were a model of empathic parenting. The same scenario in the hands of a narcissistic mother would have a completely different feel. Such a mother might allow her child to command the spotlight for her egotism, thus reinforcing the child's grandiosity while at the same time seeming, in a theatrical display before the guest, to demonstrate Mom's magnanimous parenting. What Mom might portray as attentive mothering, however, in this instance would be no more than an exercise in her own grandiosity.

Another flavor of narcissistic Mom might be annoyed and unable to contain her irritation at having a rare adult conversation interrupted by her awakening child. She might ignore the child until her cries became too intrusive or attempt to rush her daughter into some activity perceived as less bothersome to Mother. This, most likely, would fail at this age. The child's attempts to capture this mother's attention would probably evoke an angry, shaming response peppered with demands for more mature behavior. Power struggles would ensue, with the angry child demonstrating her ability to seriously disrupt an otherwise pleasant afternoon. One narcissistic mother would fail to consider the child's real needs and instead use her to inflate her own narcissistic balloon, while the other would socialize with a heavy hand and no accommodation to her child's age-appropriate needs and behavior.

The practicing and rapprochement phases of ages ten to thirty months are the point at which a narcissistic mother who has formed an earlier symbiotic bond with her child has the power to amplify her child's narcissism, creating a future Narcissist. If she rewards the child's natural grandiosity and omnipotence because it pleases her, if she fails to urge him gently into a more realistic self-image, the separation-individuation process stops. Instead of helping him see himself more realistically, she encourages him to depend for self-esteem on a fantasy version of himself as special and powerful, just as she does. He remains stuck in the narcissistic position, an extension of his mother just as she is of him.

Since the narcissistic mother has no tolerance for shame, she is unable to weather the necessary storms of the separation-individuation process, when children's behavior often causes parents considerable chagrin. When he defies her will or embarrasses her publicly, she overreacts with rage and blame. She shares her child's inability to neutralize shame, so she can't help him over this developmental hurdle either. Empathy and the ability to control aggression are never modeled by the mother or mastered by the child, who remains acutely sensitive to Mother's hostility. The child who is least able to manage shame, develop compassion, or contain aggression is the one most likely to become a Narcissist. Like mother, like child.

The Narcissistic Father

Due to her traditional role as the primary caregiver in early childhood, it is the direct impact of a mother's narcissism on her child's sense of Self that is usually most significant. But under circumstances when the child forms the symbiotic attachment to a father—when Father is the primary caretaker—his narcissism would be no less an obstacle to healthy development than a mother's, and for the same reasons.

Even in traditional households, however, a father's narcissism may indirectly influence a child in the first two years, depending on how he treats the child's mother. Mothers of young children are drained both physically and emotionally by their children's needs, and a supportive partner is an essential source of replenishment. When Father is too self-absorbed to nurture Mother, she may turn to her child to meet her own emotional needs, which may make her so "close" to the child that separation-individuation will be compromised. Children with narcissistic fathers and clinging mothers often remain bound to their mothers in unhealthy ways throughout their lives.

By the time the child reaches the last leg in her journey to selfhood, she, too, needs her father's help to complete the process of psychological separation from Mother. It is Father who represents the exciting world outside the tangled mass of Self and Mother that remains from symbiosis, but if he is uninterested in his child or otherwise unavailable, a vital bridge to autonomy is lost. Not all narcissistic fathers are remote and uninvolved, however. Some will take the child's growing interest in them as an opportunity to feed their own needs for power or admiration.

The narcissistic father typically approaches parenthood from one of two very different perspectives, but they have in common that they are both about "Me." On the one hand, he may have had no intention of becoming a father in the first place and may feel tricked, trapped, or otherwise manipulated into parenthood by the female who is carrying his child. As her body loses its familiar form, he may feel revulsion toward her. If she becomes less physically and emotionally able to satisfy his appetites, he may struggle with feelings of rejection, betrayed entitlement, and envy of the fetus. The shame beneath these feelings may be dumped onto her and her body in the form of critical remarks or sadistic jokes that express his rage. In extreme cases, he may even become physically aggressive toward her.

Just as narcissistic is the man who looks forward to fatherhood as a means of controlling his partner or replicating himself. This man's grandiose fantasies are fixed on a future in which his sphere of influence, and hence his importance, are expanded through the exploitation of those who, because of their dependence on him, can be dominated and molded to suit his needs. He may idealize his partner or treat her with indifference, but he seizes on fatherhood as a means to keep himself pumped up for a long, long time.

The narcissistic father may be abandoning from the outset, preoccupied with selfish pursuits and stingy with his time and personal resources. He may not adequately prepare for the financial responsibilities of becoming a father and express resentment about having to provide for a child. He may show little interest in the health and welfare of his child's mother and interact with her primarily to meet his own needs. He is "too busy" to attend prenatal classes or to be present at the time of birth, and he may abdicate most or all of the responsibilities of parenthood and feel that those who would like him to do otherwise are just trying to cramp his style. This is a man who sees diaper changing and 3:00 A.M. feedings as not part of his job description. Anything he chooses to give should be enough, and he is entitled to carry on his life without accommodation to his new role as a father. If the mother of his child is less available to meet his sexual and emotional needs, he feels justified in seeking satisfaction elsewhere. He may check in with the child every once in a while to see if there's anything there for him, but he seldom finds enough to sustain his interest.

The more controlling narcissistic father, on the other hand—the one who wants to use fatherhood to pump himself up—is anything but abandoning. He may hover over the mother and child, looking for ways to become a focal part of the action. His hypervigilance is a sign that he is feeling anxious, and what he is anxious about is that the mother-child bond has little to do with him. If he was possessive and demanding before the birth, he most certainly now feels excluded. She is attending to the baby and not to him, so instead of getting more, he's getting less. He may sulk or become even more demanding in an attempt to compete with his child. He may also compete with his partner by trying to lure the child away from her with toys or activities. Often, these are beyond the child's developmental level, revealing his lack of empathy and awareness of his child's actual capabilities. He may have other unrealistic expectations as well that are revealed in such remarks as, "Why doesn't she look happy to see me when I come home?"

Fathers are important to their children from birth and, if closely involved in their daily care, can connect with them, in their own masculine way, as intimately as mothers do. However, in terms of the development of a separate sense of Self, there is only one symbiotic relationship, and it is usually with Mother. While Father may feel a bit like an outsider for a few months, he does have a part to play in the separation-individuation process, and it's no less important than Mother's. Symbiosis, like childhood narcissism, is supposed to be a transitional phase, and Father's role, when the time is right, is to show his child the world beyond her private paradise with Mother. When the child is psychologically ready, there is a new lure to adventure, driven not by infantile fantasies of grandiosity and omnipotence, but by the very real prospect of mastery. The child at this phase is growing more capable by the day and ready to loosen the moorings from the Mother ship. It is Father who invites her to explore the water, and together with Mother, guides her until she can swim on her own.

Unfortunately, this process is sabotaged when Father is a Narcissist. As the child in the earliest phases of separation-individuation becomes very responsive to his stimulating interactions, the narcissistic father gets a taste of what symbiosis was like for Mother. Suddenly, he has a chance to be the child's "favorite," and he may become very possessive and compete with Mother in order to pump himself up. If Father continues in this vein, however, the power struggles of the twos and threes will be all the more dramatic, and the child will have great difficulty bringing her infantile grandiosity in line with reality. But as long as she resonates with his fantasies, the narcissistic father doesn't care. He may so revel in his child's budding efforts at autonomy as she shows more opposition toward Mother that he may fail to set limits and be reluctant to discipline her, unless her egocentrism clashes with his own. At these times, he may become excessively demanding, controlling, or critical and overly shaming of "bad behavior." And when he treats his child this way, he thinks he is exercising his paternal prerogative.

It is important to note that all parents of young children feel at times depleted, exasperated, overwhelmed, and perplexed by the considerable demands of parenting. They have feelings toward their children that they are ashamed of, and they do things they regret. This does not make them Narcissists. There are no perfect parents, and to think there are is itself a narcissistic conceit. There *are* narcissistic parents, however, and they are the ones who cannot empathize with their children, or consistently attune or respond to their children's real needs because of preoccupations with their own. There is a pervasive quality of grandiosity and entitlement that infuses such parents' behavior, and an overriding denial of reality that arises from their own needs for perfection, to idealize and be idealized by their offspring. They impose unrealistic expectations, and they are flexible only when it suits them. Their message is, "If I will it, it should be so."

The real cutting edge of parenting—especially with young children—is on the fine blade of knowing how and when to accept developmentally appropriate behavior that would be unacceptable in older children while also helping a child move forward at his or her own pace. To err on one side is to stunt the child's psychological separation and individuation, while to err on the other is to encourage the development of a false Self.

The "Pseudomature" Child

The "pseudomature" child is the one who seems to have skipped right over childhood. If you could travel back in time to observe such individuals from about the age of two or three, you might see a "little man" or a "little mother" who, accommodating to a parent's narcissistic proclivities, essentially raised him- or herself while trying to meet nearly impossible parental demands.

Researchers have shown that mothers of such children discourage them from "acting like a baby" and push them to behave more like a "grown-up," even in early childhood. They want words instead of physical contact and dislike it when their children act out anger. The kids are not supposed to make Mother feel bad if she has to leave them in someone else's care, nor are they supposed to feel—let alone express—the rage, humiliation, and powerlessness that are normal in young childhood.

Not surprisingly, children who have been given these messages and have not been helped to develop skills for managing their shame, rage, and aggression turn out to be very appealing to adults on the one hand, but on the other, they're more emotionally fragile than they initially appear. Their craving for admiration makes them clever at capturing the spotlight, but they need to be "the best," in command, winners of any competition. They are precociously self-sufficient and adept at avoiding frustration, but when they can't they fall apart, screaming, sobbing, even lashing out aggressively. They hate being helped by anyone, especially other kids, whom they tend to dominate. They are far too charming to be called "spoiled brats," but they have considerable unresolved infantile narcissism, and they desperately need to be in control to maintain their self-esteem.

Both the "pseudomature" child and the "entitlement monster" are products of narcissistic parenting. The latter is held captive in a parent's narcissistic bubble, while the former is forced out prematurely and forms a false Self that appears more competent than it actually is. Both fail to separate from their emotionally bankrupt mothers, and they become what Mother, or Father, needs them to be rather than who they truly are. Their fragile self-esteem depends on the validation of others, but they also fear dependency and intimacy, which threaten to expose their weakness and intolerable shame. They strive to be recognized as superior and may envy those who have what they do not. While they may be superficially charming, they often have a deep cold streak or a powerful hunger that comes from never having known empathic love. Those who are least able to tolerate shame and who have had their infantile grandiosity and omnipotence amplified will become Narcissists, while a larger group remain shame-driven, curiously drawn to those who resemble a narcissistic parent, and confused about what's real and what isn't. It is this group that are most in need of the survival strategies outlined in Part III, Defending Your Self.

Defending Your Self

Survival Strategies for a Narcissistic World

10

Strategy One

Know Yourself

THE ATTITUDES AND BEHAVIOR exhibited by Narcissists can stir up many different kinds of feelings in the people whose lives they touch. When you interact with these individuals, their distortions of reality can cause you to question yourself and doubt your own perceptions. Their shamelessness, arrogance, and sense of entitlement can make you angry and resentful. The way they deal with envy may cause you to feel diminished, and their rage, exploitation, and poor interpersonal boundaries may leave you feeling frightened, helplessly vulnerable, or even violated.

How you react to a Narcissist is largely determined by your previous encounters with such characters. If one or both of your parents were very narcissistic, if you were subjected to significant taunting or shaming by a sibling, if you were a shy or passive child who was exploited or abused by other children, or if you've had intimate relationships or job circumstances wherein your trust has been violated or you've felt used

by Narcissists, then you may be more sensitive than people who have not had these experiences. Our social history from the very beginning teaches us what to expect from others and how we are to feel about ourselves. That is why our number-one tool for dealing with the Narcissist is to examine our own experiences and recognize how our reactions contribute to our discomfort. The goal is to understand what is happening and interrupt the process to protect ourselves.

This is easier said than done. Our reactions to Narcissists are often very complex, and not always negative. Sometimes we are drawn to their larger-than-life qualities and the special way they make us feel when we are included in their grandiosity and omnipotence in some way. If being part of their lives makes our own seem fuller or more exciting, we may choose to pay the price or deny that there even is one. When this happens, we may end up sacrificing ourselves to an illusion that leaves us ultimately empty and bruised. When you enter the web of the Narcissist, you leave yourself behind.

The Narcissist engages us via our own narcissistic vulnerabilities. This is particularly true if we have unfinished business with a narcissistic parent. These early experiences leave us with unrealistic expectations of ourselves and a need for repair of the shame we felt when we couldn't measure up to theirs. When someone like our narcissistic parent comes along and smiles on us, it's a natural human tendency to respond to this unconsciously as an opportunity for healing. By attaching ourselves to these individuals, we get immediate gratification of our need to feel special by basking in their glow, and when we go out of our way to please them in order to hold their interest, we signal them that we can be used to meet their needs. The door is then open to the exploitation and shame-dumping that is characteristic of the way they operate. The most treacherous ones will keep us bound to them by pumping us up between the put-downs and the manipulations.

Teri is a young woman who has had more than her share of narcissistic friends and lovers, and she has also been drawn into narcissistic work environments, which you will learn more about in Chapter 17.

Teri has long had a deep hunger to be loved based on growing up with not one but two narcissistic parents, and she has also tried very hard to be someone whom others would admire. Like the Narcissist, Teri has been easily deflated and often depressed, and she has sought idealized relationships with exciting others in order to feel more interesting and important herself. Unlike the Narcissist, however, Teri is aware of her deep shame about never being good enough and can talk about it and take corrective action. When she realized why she was attracted to grandiose and omnipotent people who ultimately used her without regard for her needs or feelings, she began to make better choices for herself. In order to do this, however, she had to resist the pull of the narcissistic characters who have populated her life. It has been almost like saying no to a drug dependency, because the very people she has been using to make herself feel better are actually obstacles to her real self-esteem.

Michael came to see me because he was having panic attacks just as he started to drift off to sleep. It turned out that this happened mostly on nights when he anticipated an encounter the next morning with his boss, who sounded like a particularly toxic narcissistic personality. Michael, who held a management position that put him in the middle between the boss and several other employees, had a rescue fantasy that went back to his childhood with an alcoholic mother, and his self-esteem depended on protecting his staff from their tyrannical boss. It was an impossible task, but failure nevertheless made Michael feel weak and vulnerable. This conundrum opened the door to fears that had been locked away for many years, which Michael defended against by going into a hypervigilant, ready-to-fight mode. When he tried to sleep, his body jerked him awake in a most urgent fashion. When Michael accepted that he could not protect his staff and that the only way he could protect himself was to look for another job elsewhere, his panic attacks stopped.

Both Teri and Michael were able to disengage from their own narcissistic tendencies (the need to be perfect or in control at all times, the need to inflate a deflated self by clinging to unrealistic fantasies such as "being with this person will make me special" or "slaying this dragon will prove how powerful I am"), face their underlying shame, and make changes in their attitudes and behavior that allowed them to distance from the Narcissists who plagued them. If you find that you are frequently doing battle with or feeling seduced by such people, look to see what old problems you are trying to resolve by allowing yourself to engage in what are, essentially, impossible relationships.

Prisms and Projections

The Narcissist, too, has had experiences that explain how he or she behaves. We all view life through the lens of these experiences, but the Narcissist has something more, not just a lens but a *prism* that refracts and distorts incoming messages to avoid the intolerable feeling of shame. This means that you are never in control of how these people perceive you or when you will be assaulted with some defensive maneuver that deflects their shame, prevents their deflation, or reinflates them after a narcissistic injury.

Narcissists constantly dump—or *project*—unwanted parts of themselves onto other people. They then begin to behave as if others possess these unwanted pieces of themselves, and they may even succeed in getting others to feel as if they actually have those traits or feelings. This is an unconscious process for both the dumper and the dumpee, but what it means is that you end up being treated like the dirt they've brushed off their own psyches, or feeling the humiliation, the anger, the vulnerability, and the worthlessness that they cannot tolerate themselves. They lob it onto you, you suck it in, and for an icky while, it's yours. If you are young, dependent, or otherwise vulnerable, their "disowned" parts may stick around and become part of your own self-image. This, in fact, is the very process by which you may have acquired a vulnerability to the Narcissist in the first place.

Imagine for a moment that you are driving slowly through a parking lot at the mall when a teenager on a skateboard suddenly appears in your path, causing you to slam on your brakes. You manage to avoid hitting him, but as he sails past, he snarls and yells an obscenity at you. It is he who has been aggressive, showing by his behavior that he fails to accept that others have a right to use the parking lot, but he seems unaware of his own aggression and instead "projects" it onto you, reacting as if you are the one who has violated his entitlement to free and unobstructed access.

If you find yourself wanting to go after this young man, giving him a piece of your mind, or possibly pounding him into the pavement—and this is uncharacteristic of your usual behavior—you may have taken in and owned as yours the aggressive feelings he projected onto you. This is a common occurrence in relationships with narcissistic people, making it difficult to know sometimes why our reactions to certain situations are unusually intense.

Now imagine yourself at a dinner party, engaged in a stimulating intellectual conversation with the guest seated next to you. You seem to have much in common, and this encourages you to open up to someone who appears to be a kindred spirit. Suddenly, the temperature drops between you and she asks you where you earned your degree. Then she turns away and begins a different conversation with the person on her other side, leaving you startled and somehow embarrassed. Your kinship has come to an abrupt end, and you have no idea what happened. Chances are that something you did without even being aware of it deflated her, and you "caught" her deflected shame. Most of us have our own vulnerabilities to shaming experiences such as this, but when we cooperate with the projection and take ownership of someone else's shame, there is often a sense of unreality about what has just happened. We may realize that we have been treated with contempt, but we generally don't recognize that we have absorbed the shame of the person who is humiliating us, a shame that has been "bypassed" and kept from awareness.

These are the processes that make encounters with Narcissists so uncomfortable and confusing. It truly is difficult to know what is about the other person and what is about you. The healthier you are, the more you are able to examine your own shame, and the more you will be able to figure out which of your buttons have been pushed. If you have difficulty accessing your own feelings or accurately reading others, you may wish to consult with a therapist about this. You cannot control what others do, but you can learn to contain your own reactions once you understand what is going on. Understanding where your feelings originally came from and accepting them as your own is the first step in protecting yourself against the toxic effects of narcissism. When you become comfortable with your own feelings, you will be able to deflect the shame that is triggered by the Narcissist's internal prism.

Guidelines for Survival

1. Be aware of your feelings when in the company of someone who repeatedly evokes shame, discomfort, anger, and especially idealization in you or other people. These feelings can be excellent indicators that you are in the presence of a Narcissist. Once you have recognized whom you are dealing with, you will be in a better position to defend yourself.

2. When you have uncomfortable or intense feelings in the presence of a Narcissist, ask yourself what buttons of yours are being pushed. Remember times past when you have felt this way and, from this more emotionally distant perspective, consider why you respond as you do. Don't be afraid to look at your own narcissistic vulnerabilities, because this is exactly what will make you stronger.

3. Once you're pretty sure you've identified the piece of the action that is yours, think about how your feelings help the Narcissist manage shame in some way. Try not to personal-

ize what is happening. Although it couldn't feel more personal, it really is not. You are just a means to an end.

4. You need to find a way to detach from the feeling of diminishment the Narcissist evokes in you. Sometimes it helps to think of this person as being two years old on the inside.

5. When deflecting the shame projected by the Narcissist, resist the urge to retaliate. Don't try to challenge or enlighten this person either. The Narcissist has a lot at stake in keeping unconscious processes unconscious. If you try to tamper with this, you may escalate the situation to your own detriment or discomfort.

6. It needs to be enough for you to know that you have put the projections back where they belong in your own mind, regardless of how the Narcissist sees the situation. If you have trouble letting that be enough, you may need more personalized assistance to work on this in greater depth. A competent therapist can help.

11

Strategy Two

Embrace Reality

UNREALITY IS THE HALLMARK of narcissism. Whether it's idealizations, expectations of perfection, manufactured images, illusions, distortions of fact, catastrophizing or other kinds of exaggerations, denial, or outright lying, Narcissists will go to great lengths to avoid any reality that evokes shame and to promote fanatasies that sustain their grandiosity and omnipotence. They require accomplices for this, people to admire them and do their bidding, and often we are all too willing to meet their needs. What draws us into their web is our own longing to feel more worthwhile, more alive. Just as they need us to regulate their intolerable shame, we may need them to fill an emptiness of our own.

Except for those who are truly masochistic, no one goes into a relationship with a Narcissist looking to be demeaned, insulted, or scapegoated. No one wants to feel invaded, exploited, or afraid. No one longs to be around someone whose ego is as fragile as eggshell or who flies into a rage when thwarted. So why do so many Narcissists float like cream to the top of the social order? Why are they so prominent among our elected officials, sports idols, and entertainment figures, where we pump them up at our own expense? Why do they head large corporations and lead flocks of the faithful? Why do women swoon over arrogant men and men worship vain, shallow women?

What makes us vulnerable to the seductive allure of the Narcissist is our own need for inflation. If our self-esteem is a little shaky, if there is something missing from our lives, the Narcissist can offer a potent antidote.

Charlene grew up wanting to be a doctor like her powerful father, but a college romance that led to marriage and motherhood landed her in nursing instead. For many years, she worked in the trenches of her profession until one day she found herself the head nurse on a specialized unit of a prestigious hospital. Smart, savvy, and extremely hardworking, she came to the attention of the hospital's CEO, a charming and ambitious man who used praise to manipulate his employees into making his grandiose dreams come true. When an administrative position became available in her department, Charlene was tapped for the job. Little did she realize, however, what a price she would pay for becoming a key player on the hospital's dream team.

Over time, the jobs kept piling onto Charlene's capable shoulders. When the budget got tight and the CEO didn't want to sacrifice programming, Charlene kept saying yes to additional responsibilities to help maintain the hospital's outstanding reputation. By the time she was regularly working sixty or more hours a week, it was not just her job that had grown. In four years, Charlene had gained seventy pounds and a Motrin habit. Her large office, which became a second home, was stacked from floor to ceiling with paperwork. She rarely took more than a few days of vacation, and her personal life had all but ceased to exist. Her boss, however, couldn't say enough about her as he layered on the titles. The opportunity to be an important part of his grandiose fantasy was her reward for a life drained dry by work.

We've all known people like this who give themselves over to someone else's vision. When that someone is a Narcissist, what the devoted believe is filling them up only makes them emptier, and as time goes on, it becomes necessary to embrace the unreality in order to justify the sacrifice. It's enough to make you sick.

Barbara came to me with the sleep and appetite problems, the hopelessness and helplessness that are the unmistakable signs of depression. Young, well-educated, articulate, and attractive, Barbara should have been able to convert her considerable assets into a fulfilling life, but instead, she was struggling to end a marriage to a man she didn't respect and working in a job she hated, and she had medical problems that never seemed to get fixed. She appeared to be stuck in her misery, unable to make decisions that would put her on a more positive path. It took a while, but I finally found out why.

Barbara had a secret lover, a married man who was the center of her universe. This man and his wife were pillars in their community, and their idealized marriage was part of their mystique and their effectiveness at their work. Barbara was convinced, however, that whatever love they had once felt for one another had long since died, and she described how her lover and his wife lived very separate lives except when their public image required them to appear united. Barbara believed in the importance of the work they did and could sympathize with why it was difficult for her lover to leave his marriage. What she didn't understand was how much of her own life she was sacrificing, not just for love but to help this man maintain his inflated and false public image.

Barbara's stories of her own unsatisfactory marriage were skewed to the negative as it became impossible for her to evaluate realistically her husband's merits when she compared him to her idealized lover. She divorced him, partly because he had become a pariah to her and partly as a signal to her lover that she was ready to move their relationship to the next level. But when her lover did not take similar steps to free himself, she was devastated. She couldn't even tend to her job situation because her whole life was on hold, waiting to see if her lover would end his marriage. It was not until she had surgery and a lengthy period of recovery that she realized the full impact of her dilemma. She was "there" in every way for a man who could not even care for her in her time of need.

Barbara left treatment before her situation was resolved, so I never learned whether her lover made her dreams come true or whether she ultimately had to find her way out of the web. At the time she left, however, it was clear that she had so collapsed herself into her lover's narcissistic lifestyle that she had lost much of what she needed to be able to set herself free. Her idealizations had already cost her much of her young and promising life.

Guidelines for Survival

1. Instead of hitching your wagon to the star of a Narcissist, find your own dream. No matter how exciting they seem to be, steer clear of Narcissists and the unreality that surrounds them. The more you get caught up in their fantasies, the more you lose yourself.

2. See people for who they are, not who you want them to be. Idealization of others serves an important function at various times throughout life, but it is childlike thinking—not to mention potentially dangerous—to insist on someone's goodness, or good intentions, when that person is exploiting or hurting you. The issue is not whether someone is good or bad but whether you can deal with that person's particular shortcomings. The impact of the bad will not go away just because you don't want to face it.

3. Learn to accept that if a Narcissist lies, cheats, disrespects or hurts others, betrays confidences, takes advantage, or shows a lack of compassion, sooner or later you can expect to be on the receiving end of that same behavior.

Don't fall into the trap of thinking that something special about your relationship will spare you. That fantasy is evidence that you are caught in the narcissistic web and a signal to return to reality. If you must trust a Narcissist who behaves badly, trust that person to behave in narcissistic ways rather than to be "true to you."

4. Don't go into a relationship with a Narcissist thinking you are going to change that person, or that he or she will change because of feelings for you. Although people do sometimes change as a result of experiences in relationships, this requires something that the Narcissist lacks, the capacity to respond to compassion with compassion.

5. It is good to dream from time to time, but if you're inclined to take long vacations from the real world, you may return to find that someone has broken in and ransacked your life while you were away. The best defense against the intrusions and exploitations of the Narcissist is a good solid grasp on your own narcissistic vulnerabilities and an appreciation of your own assets. Practice living in reality and striving to make that as rewarding as your own gifts allow. If you can't control your own grandiosity or your need to idealize, you may be standing in the way of your own happiness.

12

Strategy Three

Set Boundaries

WE ALL GET ALONG MUCH BETTER when we create and respect good boundaries between one another. We've become more sensitized to the concept of boundaries as a result of our growing awareness of such problems as sexual harassment and some of the more subtle forms of child abuse, but the kind of boundaries that the Narcissist routinely violates may be more difficult for us to recognize, particularly if we weren't taught good boundaries while we were growing up.

Recall if you will that the Narcissist is developmentally arrested before having achieved the ability to see Self as separate from The One Who Meets My Needs. Internally, these individuals remain in a state of psychological fusion with that all-powerful, all-nurturant caregiver, and this becomes the working model for their interactions with others. They treat people as if they exist only to meet their needs, and they have little regard for anyone who can't be used in some way. In a psychological sense, they don't really "see" anyone else, except when a person can do something for them. They may have developed well in other regards, may be smart, funny, accomplished, even lovable, but you will sense that quality of childlike narcissism by the way they relate to the people around them. There will be inevitable violations of boundaries. More than vanity, arrogance, self-absorption, or any of the other traits we commonly think of as narcissistic, this is your biggest clue to another person's narcissism. Ignore it at your own risk.

Many boundary violations are so egregious as to be obvious to nearly everyone, such as crimes against persons or property. Others are more subtle and may even seem "normal," especially if you came from a family where separateness felt threatening or was discouraged. For example:

> Did you have a sibling who was allowed to take your toys, clothes, or other personal items, such as cosmetics or toiletries, without asking?

> Did you have a sibling who was allowed to get away with teasing or physically taunting you?

> Did a parent routinely pick your clothes or toys for you, or order for you when you were eating out?

> Did your parents barge into your bedroom or bathroom without knocking on a closed door, listen in on your phone conversations, or read your mail or diary? Were you offered choices about activities such as music lessons, sports, and hobbies, or were those decisions made for you?

If these kinds of occurrences were commonplace in your family, you may have grown up unaware of the importance of personal boundaries and unprepared to defend yourself. As you became an adult, other challenges awaited you. For example:

> Have you had friends or relatives who make a habit of stopping by uninvited, coming early for parties, going through

your medicine cabinets or closets, repeatedly asking for favors that make you feel uncomfortable, or expecting you to drop what you're doing to help them in a pinch? How about someone who doesn't want to share you with anyone else, even your spouse or children, and acts hurt if not included in most or all of your social activities? Or one who often buys the same or similar clothes, cars, homes, or home furnishings?

Does your spouse regularly open your personal mail or go through your purse, wallet, or pockets without your permission? How about reading your private journal behind your back or screening your phone calls when you'd rather he or she didn't? Has your spouse ever thrown away any of your treasured personal possessions without your permission?

Do roommates or members of your family routinely take money from your wallet or purse, or help themselves to your clothes or personal items without asking? Do they borrow your car without your permission?

Do relatives or friends give you unsolicited advice about how to raise your children? Or clean your kitchen or bathroom, do your laundry, or rearrange your furniture without consulting you first?

Has a relative or friend ever demanded to know how you invest your money, how much you spent on your car, house, or vacation, or how much you have in the bank?

Has any family member, significant other of a close friend, or person in a position of power over you ever approached you in a sexual or romantic way?

Have you had a neighbor who monitors your comings and goings, peeks in your windows or over your fence, interacts with your pets when you're not home, or leaves personal possessions on your property?

Does your boss routinely expect you to give up your lunch period or breaks, stay late, or take work home? Has anyone at work ever gone into your office or through your desk when you weren't there (other than with your knowledge and permission)?

Do other people touch you, ask you questions that are too personal, make unsolicited comments about your appearance, speak for you without your permission, or argue with you about how you feel?

These are all examples of boundary violations that most of us have experienced to some extent. Sometimes these things happen for an acceptable reason or are isolated events uncharacteristic of a given relationship. But Narcissists do these things routinely, and they do them thoughtlessly and with an absolute conviction of entitlement. Their needs are more important than yours, they know better than you do, and they would be insulted to learn that you find them intrusive or inconsiderate. The Narcissist is unlikely to self-correct this behavior just because you call attention to it. In order to protect yourself, you will have to set boundaries.

Guidelines for Survival

1. When setting boundaries, the operational word is *Control*—and we're talking about *yours*. Since you're up against someone who may be far more comfortable with exercising control than you are, think carefully in advance about how you want to proceed. What do you most want to accomplish and in what time frame? What have you tried in the past with this person, and what has and has not worked? What, if anything, is different now? Has there been a change in the power balance between you and the Narcissist? Will that work in your favor or against you? Are there others whom you might enlist to help you? Is it better to operate directly or indirectly? How do you plan to enforce your boundary? Be realistic, but also remember that there are very few situations in life where you are truly powerless. Usually, there is some-

thing you can do to improve your lot, but it is important to consider all your options first and then be willing to act.

2. Depending on the nature of your relationship with the Narcissist, which of you has more real power, and how much you are willing to risk, you may or may not want to confront the problem directly. Ordinary assertiveness techniques are often ineffective with Narcissists, because they take it as an assault on their specialness, grandiosity, and entitlement for you to bring to their attention that you are not, in fact, an extension of them and that something they have done, or not done, has upset you. You can also be sure that any confrontation of their dysfunctional behavior will disturb their need to be seen as perfect, evoking shame and its defenses. So if you care about preserving the relationship, you will need to find the gentlest way possible to deliver your message and then deftly repair the shame. Be firm and matter-of-fact, but also kind and respectful. Go ever so lightly with the empathy, however, as this often backfires when perceived as condescending. It's a good idea to practice what you plan to say with someone you can trust. Hearing yourself speaking the words will give you confidence, and objective feedback will help you polish your "presentation."

3. It is wise to work through any anger you have toward this person before making your approach. Focus on how much better you will feel when you have taken the necessary steps to protect yourself. Avoid impulsiveness and the urge to retaliate for past wrongs done to you. As satisfying as it may feel in the moment to "unload," to do so involves a loss of control you can't afford. Choose the time and place thoughtfully, and try to remain calm, even, and emotionally detached, as you would if you were setting limits with a small child. You will need your wits about you to respond to the Narcissist's reaction to your boundary-setting.

4. Be prepared for changes in the relationship other than the ones you are requesting. The Narcissist must find some way to cope with the fact that you are taking control of your own life, as this very well may upset his or her internal equilibrium. There may be testing of you in other aspects of the relationship to see how far you are willing to go to create separateness and "be your own person." There may be distancing from you and a redirection of control elsewhere, which may even feel like a loss. There may be manipulation, coercion, or efforts to seduce you into rescinding the boundaries and restoring the power this person has had over you. All of this may be very strange and challenging if you haven't been through it before. Take it slowly, think about what you are feeling and what is happening, and plan your responses carefully. Try not to fall into old traps.

5. Once you have set a boundary, keep it. If you back down, you show the Narcissist that you do not need to be taken seriously. You may have to remain forever vigilant in your interactions with this person, but the space you are protecting is where you will create your own health and happiness.

13

Strategy Four

Cultivate Reciprocal Relationships

ONE OF THE BEST WAYS TO COPE with Narcissists is to avoid becoming very involved with them in the first place. And when you can't avoid them, try to limit your involvement and surround yourself instead with healthier people who are capable of give-and-take relationships. Along the same lines, you might also want to avoid the toxic environments in which Narcissists thrive and instead seek those in which differences between people are recognized and accepted, healthy boundaries are maintained, and expectations are clear and realistic.

If you come from a narcissistic family, you will have to work especially hard to accomplish these goals. You can be sure that a parent's narcissism has left its mark on you. You may feel unworthy of relationships in which people actually value and respect you, and you may be unfamiliar with the rhythms of reciprocity. Do not despair. With insight, effort, and self-control, you can overcome these obstacles from your childhood and live in health. You may even be able to do this while maintaining relationships with the Narcissists in your family, but this will be difficult and constantly challenging. If continuing to interact with these people while you are trying to get your own life on track seems overwhelming, you may need to distance yourself, at least for a while.

It has been said that friends are the family we choose. If narcissism describes key members of your clan, it will be especially important to choose your friends wisely—and that goes double for love relationships that include physical intimacy. The tendency is to recreate the dramas of our earlier life in an effort to write new endings, but if we approach these reparative relationships without awareness or a firm grasp on reality, and with an inability to set limits, we are likely to have the same outcomes as before. If, on the other hand, we understand our vulnerabilities, see clearly through the illusions of our desires and the distortions of our fears, and find the courage to protect ourselves from those who would use us without regard for our separateness, we can change the course of our own lives. Choosing healthy friends and lovers is a very good place to begin.

What Is a Reciprocal Relationship?

1. In a reciprocal relationship, each person contributes something and each person benefits in some way. The contributions and benefits need not be spelled out or exactly equal, but it is important that each person feels he or she is receiving good value in exchange for what is offered.

2. There is flexibility in the roles of giver and taker. Whether it is an unspoken intuitive understanding, a formal contract, or something in between, there is a mechanism by which each person knows when to give and when to receive. Over the course of the lifetime of

the relationship, both parties have a sense of fairness about this aspect of their interactions.

3. Both parties are able to feel valued for their contributions and to express appreciation for what is received.

4. Separateness and boundaries are valued on both sides. In the event of conflict, both parties attempt to work out their differences with respect for one another's feelings and points of view.

5. There is no need to "keep score." Scorekeeping—keeping track of who's done what and who "owes" whom—is an indicator that someone feels the relationship is not reciprocal or has difficulty with the sometimes irregular flow of give and take.

If you come from a relatively healthy family, many of these considerations are probably second nature to you. While you may have some buttons that get pushed from time to time (no one's "wonder years" were perfect), you are less likely to project and distort and probably less vulnerable to resonating with the projections of others. In short, you probably have pretty good boundaries and little need to live in a fantasy world. Where those who have been exposed to excessive narcissism in their early years may have inherited an internal prism, you may be fortunate enough to have little that obstructs you from reading or hearing others accurately. Because you have a realistic view of yourself (both strengths and weaknesses) and the ability to empathize, you can "put yourself in others' shoes" and see them in a balanced way. Your personal life is relatively free of interpersonal strife because you tend to choose relationships with other healthy people.

If you come from health but are encountering unhealthy narcissism, it is probably in the work environment or some other place where the people you deal with are not necessarily of your choice, such as in a church, club, or other organization to which you belong. Alas, they are everywhere, and if you can't avoid them, you will have to take stock of your options, recognize any limitations and vulnerabilities you may have, be realistic about whom you are dealing with, and set those boundaries. Be grateful that you have reciprocal relationships in the rest of your life to counterbalance the narcissism that inevitably crosses all of our paths in today's world. Others less fortunate pay dearly to achieve the self-esteem that was a gift from your healthy family.

In Part IV, "Special People," we will be revisiting these coping strategies in more depth as they apply to circumstances in which narcissism can be particularly troublesome. In Chapter 14, we will look at adolescence as a kind of second toddlerhood, when some displays of narcissism are normal and some are distinctly not. Do you think you know the difference? Find out what the experts have to say, and see how good a judge you are of teenage behavior.

Addictive behavior often begins in adolescence, when brain and character development are put to the test by the biological and social challenges of maturation. Those with pre-existing deficits share a unique intolerance to shame that forms an intriguing link between narcissism and addiction. In Chapter 15, you will learn how ruptures in the family and in the development of a Self can lead to addiction and may even predict a particular drug choice. Is your Narcissist also an addict? Could you be co-dependent?

Our search for love and intimacy brings us face to face with the quality of our earliest attachments to the primary caregiver. Whether we felt safe and loved, how we resolved our own childhood narcissism, and whether we established psychological autonomy set the tone for intimate relationships throughout life. Sensations of being inflated, fantasies of ideal love, primitive longings to merge—is it love, or is it narcissism? Find out in Chapter 16.

Many of today's work environments have become stressful places where narcissistic leadership has toxic consequences for all employees. Since Narcissists seek power as a way of pumping themselves up and off-loading shame, we are most likely to encounter the boldest and most ruthless among them wherever there's a piece of turf to be controlled. Chapter 17 explores behind the mask of omnipotence to the vulnerabilities that drive Narcissists and make life miserable for those under their thumb. If you want to stay in the game, here are some tips for how to hold your own.

If you thought a narcissistic Mom or Dad was difficult while you were growing up, just wait to see what's in store when the aging process slowly and relentlessly robs them of their usual defenses. Chapter 18 is for every ACON (Adult Child of a Narcissist) who still holds out hope—as time runs out—of being seen as separate and valued in a parent's eyes. How much can you give in a relationship that offers so little reciprocity? The aging Narcissist will put you to the test.

PART IV

"Special People"

The Narcissists in Your Life

14

Adolescent Narcissism: What's Normal, What Isn't

THERE'S SOMETHING ABOUT ADOLESCENCE that seems to push adult buttons. Let's be honest and say that some of it has to do with envy—adolescents have in abundance those qualities we have valued and are losing as we age, and the very presence of their youth, energy, and promise can make us feel diminished. It would help soothe our own narcissistic wounds if they would treat us with deference and show an interest in what we care about, but too often it feels as if we are second-class citizens in a world of their making, irrelevant except to service their needs and be objects of their derision. To those of us who have been on the receiving end of someone else's narcissism, it all seems very familiar. Do you suspect your child is a Narcissist?

"Where Is the Little One I Cared For?"

Any bewildered parent of an eleven- or twelve-year-old can tell you about the child who used to like to hang out with Mom or Dad in the kitchen or the garage, who shared confidences and silly jokes, who hunkered in for a kiss or a cuddle, and then one day just stopped talking civilly to anyone outside a two-year radius and became moody, incomprehensible, and completely self-absorbed. When puberty hits, parents may have cause to wonder if their precious offspring have been invaded by body snatchers from an MTV video. What's happening here, and should you be alarmed about this sudden appearance of what looks like narcissistic behavior?

First of all, there are some hormones speaking, and that's normal. Puberty begins when a part of the brain called the hypothalamus tells a tiny gland called the pituitary to send a wake-up call to the sleeping sex organs, the testes and ovaries, to boot up and start production. Hormonal surges—especially of the male hormone testosterone (which females also secrete in smaller quantities)—cause some of the hair-trigger emotions we see in teenagers, as well as the quick shifts from feeling on top of the world to crashes in confidence that are so achingly typical, particularly in younger teens. But that's only part of the picture.

Although the ebb and flow of hormones and their accompanying feeling states will continue throughout life, to the young teen, this new intensity is all very unfamiliar and powerful. Even so, chances are the overall emotional tone has less to do with the hormones themselves than with the psychological impact of so many visible physical changes. Beginning anywhere between eight and fourteen (earlier for girls than boys), a growth spurt takes place that starts in the extremities and works its way inward to the torso, making kids look, for a period of time, as if they're all arms and legs. By ten to twelve, their voracious appetites cause fat to accumulate, and they start to become noticeably heavier. Then comes a height spurt that burns up some of the stored fat and redistributes the rest into distinctive male and female forms. The typical girl of ten to fourteen gains about thirty-eight pounds and nearly ten inches; for boys, it's forty-two pounds and ten inches between the ages of twelve and sixteen.

While they're morphing into much larger creatures with breasts or facial hair (and suffering pimples in the process), kids are convinced that everyone is looking at them with scorn. The result can be a chronic state of humiliation that evokes a repertoire of defensive behavior and attitudes. When you see evidence of those Seven Deadly Sins, think shame management.

At the same time that all these physical and emotional changes are taking place, their minds continue to develop as well. Most adolescents have been capable of logical thought since the middle of elementary school, but in the teens, they blossom into abstract thinkers who can hypothesize and use deductive reasoning as well. Now, they are able to draw specific conclusions from their expanding general knowledge, and flexing the mind is as enjoyable as chasing each other around the schoolyard or dangling from the monkey bars once was. In a more sophisticated version of the one-year-old child's love affair with the world, teenagers have a love affair with dreams and ideas—especially their own.

It is rather ironic that the newly developing ability to think deductively requires adolescents to imagine outside their own experience, because everything about themselves and their world colors the way they look at things. Egocentrism becomes as normal a part of adolescent thinking as it once was when they were toddlers, and with a similar adaptive purpose. They are gearing up to take on new roles and responsibilities, and if they can't conceive of themselves as powerful and wonderful, it might be too overwhelming.

It is common for teenagers to focus on themselves to the exclusion of others, believing, for example, that their thoughts, feelings, or experiences are unique and that they are more important in the overall scheme of things than they actually are. As if they were always performing before an imaginary audience, younger adolescents in particular are prone to speculation about what others might be thinking (especially about them), and because they are so egocentric, they are convinced that what they assume to be true actually is.

Egocentrism and deductive reasoning in adolescents form a volatile mix, leading to two types of fantasy thinking that smack of narcissistic omnipotence and grandiosity. One is called the invincibility fable, the belief that one is immune from what is dangerous to others, and the other is called the personal fable, the fantasy of being unique, heroic, or even mythical.

"I'm King of the World!"

The invincibility fable is what allows some teens to engage in risky behavior—smoking, drinking, drug use, unprotected sex, extreme "sports," dangerous driving, or even criminal activity—with little or no fear of consequences. Parents often wonder how their otherwise intelligent children can be so just-plain-dumb. But their fearlessness is not just foolhardy—it also has an adaptive component. Just as the one-year-old needed to feel invincible in order to begin exploring his surroundings, the adolescent on the brink of adulthood must feel confident enough to take on more adult challenges and develop more grown-up levels of competency. Feeling invincible neutralizes crippling doubt.

Ben is an example of a boy who is pushing this envelope. Always a daredevil, he began skateboarding at six and before long was doing stunts that even the older kids wouldn't try. At ten, he took his athletic prowess to the ski slopes and began to surf the half-pipes on a snowboard. By the time he was sixteen, Ben had entered the elite group of "extreme" boarders who defy death while leaping off cliffs with only an edge of metal and an attitude between themselves and an early grave. His mother, Jeannie, prays a lot and keeps current on her medical insurance premiums. Her friends think she's nuts for letting her son take such risks, but Jeannie would rather see Ben exercise his obvious natural talents than take that appetite for risk down some dead-end road. Ben has never used drugs ("He wouldn't dare!" she points out), and he is a better-than-average student who hopes someday to become an action filmmaker.

"You Couldn't Possibly Understand!"

The personal fable has all the earmarks of narcissistic grandiosity and can lead a teenager to think and behave as if he or she were somehow more special than others and destined for glory regardless of talent or effort. When this manifests as more than temporary arrogance, contempt, or entitlement, the underlying narcissism may be unhealthy. On the other hand, if fantasy serves to sustain motivation and leads to real accomplishment, this is healthy narcissism in action. Most achievements, after all, begin with a dream.

Marla has always had "big ideas" and a tendency to see herself in the spotlight. As a child, she was a natural entertainer who thrived on the attention of adults and other children alike. She loved to dress up, especially in her mother's cast-off formalwear and costume jewelry, and create make-believe scenes featuring herself in an assortment of roles. Her parents smiled on this activity and enrolled her in classes to develop her singing, dancing, and acting skills. In middle school, she began talking to agents. Wanting to provide some balance, her parents insisted that she also spend some time baby-sitting and volunteering at a nearby hospital, and she loved telling stories to the children and brightening the lives of the patients. When adolescence hit full-tilt, Marla had her share of dramatic moments and power struggles with her parents, but they were able to guide and contain her through these normal storms. Today, she is a focused and well-adjusted young woman studying at a well-known school for performing arts.

Not all children are as fortunate as Marla has been to have parents who know when to indulge and encourage and when to interrupt a child's self-centeredness with some other-directed experiences. A return to normal developmental narcissism and egocentricity in adolescence is a challenge to parents and teenagers alike. Those who are not offered opportunities to develop a broader worldview and a more realistic sense of their place in the overall scheme of things often become unhappily stuck at the center of their own narrow universe.

What kids need, well before adolescence in fact, is someone who recognizes their unique capabilities and offers encouragement and opportunity from the sidelines while they master real skills. This is quite different from wanting something specific from or for a child in the absence of any particular inclination or ability, or mindlessly repeating "You can do it!" to a child who clearly can't. It requires a kind of empathic attunement to a particular child and his or her native abilities and personal dreams.

Self-Esteem

An unfortunate trend in the way we have parented and educated children in recent years has focused on the inculcation of "self-esteem" as a primary goal. While nearly everyone would agree that it's important for children to feel good about themselves, and even that self-esteem provides some immunity from the ravages of an assortment of social ills from poverty to child abuse, inoculating children with "the social vaccine of self-esteem" has had some unintended consequences.

The first thing that happened was that the new curriculum that taught elementary-schoolers to focus within themselves on their own inherent goodness crowded out some of the very skill development that would have given them something to feel good about. Children were encouraged to recite positive self-affirmations regardless of their actual performance and ended up absorbing the more subtle message that it is effort rather than accomplishment that matters and that there's something wrong with feeling "bad." If your feelings are hurt when you don't get what you want, someone or something else is to blame, and you're entitled to recourse. A sense of entitlement to "specialness" and positive outcomes has compromised rather than enhanced real self-esteem, which is based on mastery rather than wishful thinking. Such unrealistic expectations as "I can be (or have) whatever I aspire to" and "I deserve to be rewarded if I try hard" are thought to have something to do with the tenfold increase in depression in the United States in the past generation and a half, with a mean age of first onset in midadolescence.

Who Am I?

The essential task of adolescence is to complete the process begun in early childhood of forming a whole and separate sense of Self as a unique person whose behavior and attitudes are consistent across time and circumstance. In the optimal course of events, adolescents are permitted a moratorium from full adult responsibility and an increasing amount of operating room to experiment with different roles until they find the ones that fit. At the end of this process are both a strong individual identity and a sense of solidarity with the ideals of a larger group—what we call character.

A necessary and painful part of this process is the severing of infantile ties of dependence on adult authority in general and parents in particular. It is not that young people no longer need their parents—far from it—but more that they need to give up childhood and all its representations, of which the early parent-child bond is one of the most prominent.

Psychoanalytic thinkers find a remarkable resemblance between what goes on in adolescence and the separation-individuation process that unfolds in early childhood. Like the young child who is sorting out what is Self and what is Other, the young adolescent needs to differentiate psychologically from the parents and family. Both the infant and the young adolescent are propelled toward gestures of independence by quantitative leaps in physical maturity. The ensuing "practicing" period for adolescents involves a testing of newly won powers and, optimally, a greater range of freedom while still under adequate protection from parents. Even the teen's rebelliousness and irritability find parallels in the mood shifts from determined exuberance to depleted low-keyedness of the "practicing" child. And there are striking similarities between the ambivalence toward parents—at once seeking security and support, then pushing away angrily—of the early adolescent to midadolescent and the "rapprochement" child. Both struggle with fears of engulfment and loss of autonomy as they forge ahead in their quest for a separate identity. (See Chapter 8 for a full discussion of "practicing" and "rapprochement" in early childhood.)

In the second individuation phase that occurs during adolescence, love of the parent is replaced by love of the emerging Self, which to observing adults looks like the mythical Narcissus enamored of his own image reflected in the pool. Behind the scenes of adolescent self-love, however, a psychic restructuring is underway that cannot take place unless the child regresses psychologically to a more primitive and egocentric way of thinking. Regression to earlier kinds of behavior at any age is often a defense against internal fragmentation and carries with it certain risks to healthy functioning and development. But adolescent regression to the narcissistic position is both necessary and a normal crisis with inherent dangers. It allows the adolescent's more mature persona to come into contact with longings to merge and destroy in order to bring these primitive urges under self-control. On the other side of the storm is character, the function of which is to maintain internal strength and self-control, thus freeing the individual to pursue life's possibilities. By late adolescence, when character formation is complete in the healthy individual, childhood helplessness and anxiety are integrated into the adult Self and lose their power to cause continual harm and stress. This cannot happen without healthy narcissistic energy, and by the same token, healthy narcissistic gratification is the reward for having achieved character.

Unfortunately, not all teens make it through this process.

When Things Go Wrong

There are basically three things that can happen to arrest healthy identity development and perpetuate adolescent narcissism in the young adult-to-be. The first is called foreclosure, and it tends to occur when teens are too intimidated by the expectations of their families or culture to engage in normal experimentation. These are often the children of overbearing narcissistic parents who cannot tolerate the teenager's growing need for separateness and threaten the child with psychological or actual abandonment as a punishment for exercising independence. The child considers the risks and decides prematurely to do what is expected, becoming a doctor like Mom or the scientist Dad wanted to be without first engaging in a journey of self-discovery. When the parents' or culture's roles and values are adopted wholesale and without examination, the process of establishing a personal identity is short-circuited. Some of these individuals rework this struggle more successfully later in life, while others are never free from the narcissistic web and only feel good when they are pleasing someone other than themselves.

A second possibility is the formation of a negative identity in opposition to everything the child has been taught up to that point. These teens tend to feel that they are supremely independent and evolved, but the truth is that their entire identity is formed in opposition to authority instead of as an outcome of integrating that which they have been given with that which they have discovered on their own. There is no mature process of self-examination and identification with the positive values of a larger group, only an angry rejection of expectations that they find unattainable or unappealing. Often, their attitudes and behavior are fueled by a narcissistic rage based on disappointed entitlement. There may also be a considerable amount of grandiosity in this position, as opposed to the more realistic perception of Self and Other that comes from healthy identity achievement. As long as identity is based more on being against than for, the narcissism persists.

A third type of failure to achieve a mature identity is called identity diffusion, and it is a problem that can plague an individual well into adulthood. These are the young people who have few commitments to any goals or values and who often seem apathetic about taking on any role. In adolescence, they may have difficulty finishing homework, choosing a college, finding a job, or planning for their own future. They move through relationships both sexual and platonic without any sense of connection, passion, or commitment. They just don't seem to care what their identity is. The narcissism of these teens is perhaps the most primitive of all—the false Self that masks their lack of development is a deflated one, lacking in the omnipotence and grandiosity that could propel them toward some experience of mastery and definition of Self.

Narcissistic Rage and Teen Violence

Children know intuitively what is valued in the world they live in, and many of today's children know it isn't them. There is widespread concern about the emphasis in our culture on appearance, achievement, acquisition, and power, and it's no wonder that our young people want to look good, outperform their peers, get what they want right now, and "rule." They crave opportunities to measure up to cultural ideals and feel humiliated and enraged when they can't. And the saddest part of it all is that when they look to adults for guidance, for role models, for someone to listen and understand, there's no one home—literally and otherwise.

From 1978 to 1998, the percentage of American families in which both parents worked increased from slightly over 40 percent to just over 60 percent, and the number of single-parent families with working mothers also increased from just under 60 percent to 70 percent. A long-term study of seven thousand 1990s teenagers found that they spent an average of 3.5 hours alone every day. In May 1999, in the wake of the Columbine High School shooting in Littleton, Colorado, that killed fifteen people and wounded twenty-three more the previous month, Americans were bombarded with statistics such as these as the country groped for a way to bend our collective mind around the growing horror of adolescent violence, depression, and despair. *Time* magazine reported that "parents spend 40 percent less time with their kids now than 30 years ago." *Newsweek* chimed in: "In survey after survey, many kids—even those on the honor roll—say they feel increasingly alone and alienated, unable to connect with their parents, teachers, and sometimes even classmates. They're desperate for guidance, and when they don't get what they need at home or in school, they cling to cliques or immerse themselves in a universe out of their parents' reach, a world defined by computer games, TV, and movies, where brutality is so common it has become mundane."

When narcissistic parents are too absorbed with their own preoccupations to spend time with their kids, they often raise narcissistic children, or at least children with profound narcissistic vulnerabilities, such as shame-sensitivity and the inability to manage intense negative feelings or to control their own aggressive impulses. Several years ago, a study of elementary-school-aged boys showed that those who were already identified as aggressive were less skillful than their more docile peers at accurately interpreting the behavior of others their age and were more likely to read intentional hostility into an ambiguous situation and respond with a preemptive strike.

Researchers long ago showed that future antisocial behavior could be predicted in *two- and three-year-old children* on the basis of both individual traits and parental factors. Extreme restlessness in infancy, nonsubmissiveness to authority, and destructiveness were evident in very young children who later became troubled teens. And if either parent had a history of delinquency, alcoholism, or emotional disturbance and had failed to attach to the child in the early formative years, that, too, was correlated with children who would become antisocial. These are the same qualities that are evident in the developmental arrest that is pathological narcissism: impaired parents and an impaired parent-child bond, leading to children who cannot manage their own feelings or control their own behavior and who recognize no authority but their own. When children face the challenges of adolescence with these deficits already in place, it's a recipe for violence.

Guidelines for Survival: Holding the Reins on Teenage Narcissism

Strategy One: Know Yourself

Arrogant, entitled teenagers who are a law unto themselves push a lot of people's buttons. What buttons of yours do they push? What do your feelings tell you to do? Do you act on these urges? How effective have you been?

If the teenagers in question are your own, you might want to ask yourself what narcissistic traits or vulnerabilities of yours have contributed to the problem as you now understand it. It is tempting to blame society, the schools, the government, the politicians, the media, your ex-spouse, or any number of other factors outside your control, but that won't help you find solutions. Instead, it will probably make you feel helpless and angry. Better to start with what you can control—your own behavior.

- Do you clearly communicate your values and expectations to your child?

- Are you someone your child can respect, not just because you are a parent, but because of the way you have conducted your life?

- Do you show respect for your child's separateness and individuality?

- Do you know when your child really needs you, and are you available at those times?

- Do you provide adequate supervision of your child's activities?

- Do you encourage your child to think for him- or herself?

- Do you offer your child opportunities to build character?

- Do you link increased privileges and freedom to evidence of increased maturity?

- Can you admit to your child when you have been wrong?

Even though it sometimes doesn't seem like it, your children are listening to what you say and watching what you do. They need your guidance and support, even when they're pushing you away. Give the gift of character—be someone they can admire.

Strategy Two: Embrace Reality

You cannot change other people's narcissistic children, and you cannot effect changes in your own children overnight.

The world has become a much more dangerous place than it was fifty, or even thirty, years ago. There are many angry, shameless people out there with no compassion for others, and some of them are teenagers. Avoid confrontations in situations when the power balance doesn't favor you, and keep an even temper when trouble can't be sidestepped.

By the same token, do not become overly pessimistic or assume that all teenagers are hopelessly overprivileged and undersocialized. Most of them are just going through a normal phase and are doing so under circumstances that many adults can scarcely imagine. Adolescence remains for most a time of idealism, and many young people have more integrity than their parents. The fact that teen pregnancy declined throughout the 1990s, as did juvenile arrests for violent crimes in the last half of the decade, offers hope for the future. Take a look at your own community for other sources of inspiration close to home.

If you are concerned about unhealthy narcissism in your own children, realize that there will need to be changes in the way your whole family operates in order to deflate grandiosity and entitlement, soothe rage, and develop the capacity to tolerate shame. This is not just your child's problem, it is a family problem. You will need to have a plan to address each person's part in this problem, as well as a plan for anger management—yours and everyone else's. Be realistic about what can and cannot be accomplished, and in what time frame. Research your options before deciding how to proceed. Don't fall victim to your own grandiosity, perfectionism, or need to overcontrol.

Strategy Three: Set Boundaries

Do not tolerate unacceptable behavior in your own or other people's children. In the case of the latter, you may need to invoke other parents or outside authorities to protect yourself and your children. Don't hesitate to do so, even if you don't believe you'll be effective. Be as persistent as you need to to see that your concerns are properly addressed. It is important to take a stand against unhealthy narcissism, particularly in young people who may still be malleable. Teach your children to recognize and avoid narcissism and narcissistic values in their peers.

If it is your own children who seem to show unhealthy narcissism, you will need to identify what behavior is unacceptable and try to understand what the behavior means before attempting to contain it. You will not be as effective in setting limits with your children if you don't know why they act as they do. Your children will see you as arbitrary and uncaring, and they will be right. Instead, help them explore and articulate what they are feeling. Try to come to some kind of mutual understanding that frames your child's behavior in a charitable light. This is not the same as making excuses for a child's unacceptable behavior. It is a way of engaging with the child toward better self-understanding and self-control. If you search for explanations that assume good, if misguided, intentions, you can still let them know that you are disappointed in their behavior but know that they have the capacity to improve.

For example, if your son gets in trouble for fighting in school, try to help him identify what triggered his anger. If his feelings seem irrational, find out if they even make sense to him. When you've identified his feelings, then it's time to ask him if, in retrospect, he can think of any other ways he'd rather have handled his problem. Let him know that you find fighting an unacceptable way of expressing acceptable feelings. Treat his feelings with respect, and show him that you give him credit for being able to think through his problems and avoid predictable consequences, like getting suspended from school.

Or if your daughter flies into a rage when you won't let her go to the mall before her homework is finished, try to find out why she thinks it's so urgent to go now and what her plan is for getting her work done on time. Sometimes teens have a poor sense of how much can be accomplished in a particular time frame. Insisting that they do their homework first teaches them to be more realistic and to postpone gratification. Don't be afraid to set limits, but do offer your child a chance to express his or her point of view out loud to you. Hearing themselves think in the presence of someone who is calm but firm helps them develop character and more realistic perceptions. It is very important that you refrain from anger and humiliation at these times. It is also important to be genuinely connected and not emotionally detached. This is perceived as arbitrary and uncaring and will often generate rage. If you get this reaction, question your own behavior before assuming that your teen is having a hormonal moment.

When setting consequences for violations of rules, try to include your child in the process. Appeal to his or her sense of fairness and, whenever possible, try to come to an agreement, as opposed to simply invoking authority. Do not, however, abdicate your role as parent. Let your child know that you have the right to set standards for the family, that you expect compliance, and that you intend to stay involved and monitor his or her progress toward agreed-upon goals. Then do whatever is necessary to follow through. Use force only as a last resort, and only to protect life and property.

Strategy Four: Cultivate Reciprocal Relationships

It can be very difficult to develop reciprocity with a teenager who does not want to include you in his or her world except in marginal or selfish ways. You must balance the teen's need for time apart from you and the family with expectations of participation in family life. Try to remember that if your child was well-connected to you before adolescence, a return to reciprocity is likely to occur once normal adolescent narcissism has subsided.

If, on the other hand, you are just beginning to recognize a longer-standing narcissistic problem in your already-adolescent child, the way ahead is likely to be rockier. You will have to articulate your expectations to someone who is apt to ignore you or become indignant. You are essentially beginning the process that should have occurred when your child was a toddler, and you will have to be firm but compassionate to weather a more sophisticated version of the "terrible twos." Hang in there—it's worth it.

Ginny: The Good Mother

Ginny grew up the oldest of four in a family where both parents were very self-absorbed, demanding, and nonempathic with their children. She was not allowed to have an opinion, or even a feeling, of her own, and from the time her brothers were born, she had a job to do. It was she who warmed their bottles and changed their diapers when she came home from school, and she who read them stories and put them to bed at night. Her mother was always tired, and afflicted with one malaise after another. Her father was a stern and angry man who could be a tyrant if things didn't go his way. When Ginny was sixteen, she counted herself lucky to be able to work afternoons and weekends at a food bank across town. It was her chance to be part of the world outside her family home. At eighteen, she married to escape for good.

Only it wasn't good. Her husband, like her parents, controlled her completely. When the children came, one after another, it was as if she had never left home at all. Everyone had a claim on her, and when they were through with her at the end of the day, there was nothing left inside. The emptiness was unbearable, and she sought to fill it by becoming the best at the only thing she had ever known, taking care of other people. Ginny decided that she would be the best Mom she could be.

The way that Ginny would know that she was a good mother was if her children were never unhappy. So she watched over them anxiously, ready to respond to any tear, any whine, any sign at all of distress. In time, the children came to know that if they were not happy, it was their mother's fault. And their father was only too willing to agree that this was so. As they entered their teens, Ginny's daughter became so fearful that she could barely stand to have her mother leave her sight, and her son evolved into an angry, indolent loner. Ginny could see that her children were terribly unhappy, and she was consumed with guilt. Surely, she was a terrible mother after all.

So she redoubled her efforts to brighten their lives. For her daughter, this meant becoming a chauffeur and barely having a moment to herself. In her son's case, it meant buying him electronic equipment and indulging his moods. Then one day, she could stand it no longer. She decided she wanted something for herself. She wanted her children to care about her feelings and to consider her time and the money she spent on special treats as gifts rather than entitlements. It was the beginning of a revolution.

She started by insisting that her daughter get more involved with her peers, do more for herself, and find others to depend on. Ginny learned to say no to her daughter and to defend the space she created for herself. At first, there was clinging and pouting and angry outbursts, but in time, Ginny's daughter began to grow out of the nest and gain confidence in her budding social skills. She actually looked forward to outings with friends, and she even started to date. Before too long, she became thoughtful and sometimes even compassionate toward her mother.

Ginny's son was more difficult for her to handle, however. He did not like to be asked to do things on his mother's terms, and he continued to expect that all his wishes would be granted as before, automatically. Ginny began to discuss with him the concept of reciprocity. It was a new one for him. He had always believed that you did things for other people because you felt like it, not because they needed you to. The thought that "we are family and we do for one another out of caring" was utterly alien to him. It would take time to change the lifelong pattern of their relationship, but Ginny had come to understand that if she really wanted to be a good mother, she would have to teach her son to give.

In narcissistic families, some people are givers and some people are takers, but hardly anyone gets to be both. If you are unhappy with the narcissism of your adolescent children, ask yourself what values you have taught them and what examples you have set. Reciprocity is an attitude. Before you can instill it in your children, you have to believe in it yourself.

Narcissism and Addiction:
The Shame Connection

SHAME, THAT PERVASIVE SENSE of Bad Self that is at the root of all unhealthy narcissism, is among the most intolerable feelings a person can have, no matter what age or circumstance. Often we will do whatever we can to make the feeling go away as quickly as possible. What could be quicker than drugs, alcohol, or any of the other myriad ways we compulsively avoid reality? Experts in the field of addictions widely agree that chronic and pervasive shame is the feeling that drives addictive and compulsive behavior, giving narcissism and addiction an emotional link. Experiencing oneself as flawed is a deep narcissistic wound that can create an overwhelming need for mood-altering experiences.

The Ruptured Bad Self

Mitch removed his shoes at the door as he had always done, mindful not to scuff his mother's hardwood floors. Sometimes, when no one else was home, he would run and slide down the long hallway past the antique desk that she was so proud of, with the flowers arranged just so in the crystal vase that Dad had given her on their 15th wedding anniversary. God, how she fussed over those stinking flowers, like they were her babies or something. She would spend hours tending her garden and then drone on about fertilizer and pesticides. It drove him crazy. In his stocking feet, Mitch liked to fly past the roses and snapdragons and see how close he could come to the grandfather clock at the end of the hall without actually crashing into it. He especially enjoyed playing this game when he was loaded, knowing that at any moment he could bring down destruction on all that his mother held so dear.

Not tonight, however. "You're late," his father growled at him from the den. Mitch shuffled toward the flickering light coming from the TV and composed his face into a blank screen. "I don't know why I bothered to buy you a watch," his father started in. "You obviously can't tell time." "We were at . . .," Mitch began to explain when his father cut him off, as usual. "And don't try to blame those loser friends of yours," his father snarled, reaching for his martini. By now, Mitch figured, this would be about his fourth. Better to just let the old man have at him for a while, no sense fighting back. Marinated as he was in vodka and vermouth, there would be no reasoning with him, and besides, Mitch was tired and still a little high himself. It would be easy to tune Dad out. He practiced listening to the sound but not the words, as if his father were speaking a foreign language. The ranting went on for several more minutes; then Dad seemed to run out of steam. "Get out of here, you little punk," his father said. "Go to bed."

On his way upstairs, Mitch ran into his mother. "Oh, you're home, dear." She smiled cheerfully. "Come tell me all about your evening!" He sighed and followed her into her bedroom, where she plunked down on the bed and patted the spot beside her, inviting him to sit. He hated these little charades of intimacy, where she pretended to understand how he felt about everything, although he was pretty careful never to actually tell her what he was feeling at all. He had more than a suspicion that anything he might reveal to her in a moment of weakness would become gossip fodder at her next garden club meeting or luncheon with girlfriends. His mother loved to tell people how close she was to her son, how they could talk about "just anything." Their conversations usually turned to her, however, as she attempted to "relate" to whatever crumbs of information Mitch deemed it safe to part with. Tonight he just didn't feel like going through the motions. "I'm a little tired, Mom," he said, trying to avoid her eyes. "I think I'll just go to bed." Even without looking, he could feel her disappointment, and it filled him with unbearable heaviness.

Alone in his room, Mitch turned on his music, turned off the lights, and stretched out on the bed. The marijuana he had smoked earlier with his friends had worn off, and he didn't like the way he was feeling. He couldn't put words to the discomfort, but he knew that if he didn't do something about it, he wasn't going to go to sleep, and something else, something bad, might happen. What that might be, he didn't want to think about, didn't want to know. What he did know was what he could do to feel better. Without turning on the lights, he went to his closet and pulled out the box that held his dress shoes. There in the toe of his barely worn oxfords was a small stash of downers he had scored a few months back. He tossed one of the pills in his mouth and washed it down with the remnants of a can of flat soda sitting on his nightstand. Then he lay back down and waited for deliverance from the pain.

As the warm, soft feelings began to spread throughout his body, Mitch remembered the day, in eighth grade, when he had decided to try marijuana. He had always planned to "just say no," but when the moment of truth came, he felt a compelling boldness. He knew some other kids who had tried weed, and nothing bad seemed to have happened to them. Maybe all the scare stories were just a lot of grownup lies. He took a few hits and, sure enough, the world didn't come to an end. Finding ways to sneak off and share some bud with his friends gave him a little buzz all by itself, and before long, he also began to enjoy the way the drug made him feel—mellow, but at the same time powerful and in control. Not at all like his usual yucky feelings of awkwardness and self-doubt. Just like magic, Mitch had discovered that he never had to feel bad again. A single tear wet his pillow *as he slipped into sleep, enveloped in the tender embrace of the one friend he could rely on.*

The Narcissistic Family

Psychologically, addicts and Narcissists have much in common, beginning with the fact that they both come from troubled families. The kind of faulty parenting that creates an addict—like that which makes a Narcissist—features inconsistency, little or no limit-setting, and that combination of solicitousness alternating with rage that is so confusing to children. Parents who are not consistent, reliable, or trustworthy, and who do not respond adequately to the young child's developmental needs for empathic attunement, aren't supplying enough of the raw materials required to build a healthy Self—or a healthy brain.

The failure of primary caretakers to attune to a young child's feelings, to defuse emotional overloads and to amplify low-arousal states, especially after periods of separation, interferes with neurological development and can lead to such deficits as poor impulse control and low frustration tolerance. Early social deprivation and stress appear to result in permanent alterations in the brain chemistry for regulating strong emotions. When the child is deprived of empathic care during peak periods of brain development, which occur at both ends of the practicing phase (10 to 12 months, and 16 to 18 months), key areas of the brain remain immature and underdeveloped.

Unable to regulate strong feelings on their own, these individuals may turn to chemical substances as "auxiliary regulators." Essentially, they have a faulty thermostat that allows their emotional temperature to become too hot. They try to cool things down with drugs, correcting for the missing neural pathways that didn't develop properly in early childhood. The drugs act to trigger narcissistic fantasies and feelings of grandiosity and omnipotence that provide relief from shame and depression. Like the Narcissist, who compensates by bypassing shame, the addict has found a way to make up for a crucial deficit in brain development that is the result of parental misattunement.

Parents who are inconsistent, who have poor boundaries, who are self-absorbed and unavailable, also interfere with their child's moral development by failing to provide the combination of firmness and love that allows them to be used as models for conscience. Whatever moral structure these children are able to piece together in childhood often collapses in adolescence. Drugs step in to provide both a relief and a pleasure, a kind of substitute ideal that is normally supplied by the adolescent's own budding internal sense of meaning, goal-directedness, and values. Drugs become the putty that fills the gaping hole in the psychological structure when a child is deprived of a parent he or she can idealize.

The Shared Core Defect of Narcissism and Addiction

Both Narcissists and addicts share a tendency to grandiosity and omnipotence. Experts say that addicts seek to re-create that early childhood fantasy of being without limits and perfectly cared for by idealized others. If an addict encounters limits or is disappointed in a relationship, uncontrollable primitive emotions erupt. Awareness of real personal limitations triggers intolerable shame, and the perception that an idealized other is not as great and all-giving as expected leads to feelings of abandonment and loneliness. Anything short of total union is experienced as total rejection. Neither the Narcissist nor the addict is able to manage these intensely unpleasant feelings in mature, healthy ways. When the internal world of idealized Self and others collapses, the devastation can lead to a narcissistic rage of even murderous or suicidal proportions.

Like Narcissists, people who turn to drugs often need to feel a sense of omnipotent control over someone or something that meets their needs, yet they have great difficulty trusting others. Both addicts and Narcissists are impatient people who are unable to tolerate delay, which can make them exploitative in their quest for immediate gratification. Drugs allow addicts to meet their needs without exerting any psychic effort. They cannot tolerate the tension, pain, or frustration of putting their real capabilities on the line, and they seek, through drugs, to alleviate their anxieties about their own competence. Narcissists, too, have trouble activating the "real Self," and they live in a world of unreality. Ingestion of drugs allows addicts to return to that psychological state where most Narcissists live, a piece of early childhood when they felt in control of whatever soothed them.

Drug Preferences and Arrests in Separation–Individuation

The structural defects that lead to addictive and compulsive behaviors often lie dormant throughout middle childhood only to erupt in dramatic fashion in adolescence. As discussed in the last chapter, adolescence is a time of identity formation and consolidation, when the internalized attitudes, behaviors, and values of adult role models, particularly parents, are sorted, tested, and integrated or rejected to form a mature, autonomous Self. The passive experiences of earlier childhood must be converted into action in order for this adult psychological structure to take shape. For those with primitive structural defects, the normal anxieties, depressions, and physical discomforts of adolescence can be so overwhelming as to cause regression and retreat instead of growth. Childlike magical thinking may make drugs seem seductive, promising relief without the need for active mastery and adaptation.

Contrary to popular opinion, most young people today do not use drugs and alcohol, but the statistics for the last decade of the 20th century are nevertheless alarming. From 1991 to 1996, current (within the previous month) illicit drug use more than doubled for both 8th graders and 10th graders. For 12th graders, it increased by half during the same period. By 1998, more than one-quarter of all high school seniors were currently using illicit drugs, and 54 percent had tried drugs at some time in their young lives. Starting in 1997, drug use among teens began to level off and drop slightly, but it still remained at shockingly high levels. As the century came to a close, alcohol and marijuana were the undisputed drugs of choice among teens who indulged, mirroring adult patterns. Use of alcohol remained around 25 percent for 8th graders, 40 percent for 10th graders, and over 50 percent for 12th graders throughout the 1990s, while current use of marijuana involved nearly 10 percent of 8th graders, almost twice as many 10th graders, and nearly a quarter of all high school seniors in 1998.

The children who participated in these surveys of teen drug use were born in the years 1974 to 1985, when cultural narcissism and adult drug use were rampant. One quarter of American households reported illicit drug use in 1979, and from 1977 to 1987, more than one million Americans a year tried cocaine for the first time. Many more millions were affected by alcoholism, eating disorders, gambling, and other forms of addictive behavior. It should come as no surprise, then, that the children born in this generation of compulsive excesses would discover in their teens a considerable affinity for their own mood-altering experiences.

Noting that addicts often referred to their drug of choice as "mood food" or "instant Mommy," researchers in the late 1960s began to study the "regressive states" induced by different drugs and to recognize how much they resembled specific phases of early childhood development. Hallucinogens, stimulants, and narcotics each have a distinct effect that seems to re-create or reflect a primitive feeling state.

LSD and similar hallucinogens, for example, produce a loss in the sense of the boundaries of the Self. Changes in body image and the perceptions of Self and others while "tripping" lead to feelings of fusion and merger, depersonalization (a loss of the sense of Self), and delusions. Some people react with anxiety to those experiences, while others can't wait to repeat them. For those who are drawn to this pharmacologic effect, the payoff is the fantasy fulfillment of wishes for union, reunion, and fusion with lost or yearned-for others. This suggests an attempt to regain that earliest childhood state of oneness with an all-giving caretaker.

Recall the "low-keyedness" of the practicing toddler at approximately 18 months of age when Mother is temporarily absent or unavailable. The child seems to slow down and turn inward, is minimally responsive to the environment, and seems to be conserving energy. Opium and its narcotic derivatives, such as heroin, seem to produce a similar state of quiet lethargy, of decreased involvement with external reality, and a blissful satiation conducive to fantasies of omnipotence, magical wish fulfillment, and self-sufficiency. The state of opium intoxication known as "being on the nod" might be compared to this early narcissistic state.

Narcotics and barbiturates also have the power to mute underlying rage and aggression that would be too threatening or disorganizing for someone with a primitive developmental arrest to express openly. By the same token, shame, loneliness, and anxiety can be soothed away. These are precisely the feelings that the practicing-stage child is thought to hold in check in Mother's absence, for fear that she will not return.

Amphetamines, methedrine, cocaine, and other stimulants, on the other hand, seem to correspond to the active, exuberant demeanor of the toddler when Mother is present or readily available. Recall that the practicing stage is the peak period of grandiose, omnipotent childhood narcissism, before fantasies have been converted to reality and before necessary shame has been integrated by the toddler on his way to that first separate, autonomous sense of Self. These stimulant drugs increase feelings of assertiveness, self-esteem, and frustration tolerance while decreasing judgment, accuracy, and the awareness of fatigue, not unlike the boundless energy and fearless omnipotence of the toddler.

Certain individuals may use cocaine—the drug of choice for grandiose Narcissists—to amplify a hyperactive lifestyle, to reassure themselves that they are self-sufficient, and to mask an underlying depression. Stimulants in general provide a sense of aggressive mastery, control, invincibility, and grandeur that protects against feelings of unworthiness and weakness—the practicing child unmasked, as it were. Of all the types of regressive gratifications provided by drugs, the increase in self-esteem and the re-creation of a regressive narcissistic state of self-satisfaction are said to be the most consistent ones.

The vast majority of alcohol and drug use in our culture is of an experimental, casual, or recreational nature. Those who chronically seek intoxication for the relief of what bothers them and the restoration of what is missing, however, belong in another category. They are addicts. The compulsive search for mood-altering experience usually begins in adolescence, when narcissistic issues come to the fore and force the young person to confront his or her own true developmental capacities—or lack thereof. Those who carry the wounds of early narcissistic injury deep within them often find they don't have the internal "stuff" to rise to the considerable challenges of adolescence. Whether they choose drugs and alcohol as a way to neutralize their overwhelming emotions or any of the other smorgasbord of compulsive options that present themselves so abundantly in our society, the core inability to regulate their own feelings becomes the link between their narcissistic vulnerability and the road to addiction.

Guidelines for Survival: Coping with Compulsions, Mine and Yours

Compulsive and addictive behaviors are such an enormous, and often unconscious, part of the way we live today that scarcely anyone's life is untouched. In addition to alcohol, drugs, and food, we can also be addicted to feelings (such as rage, excitement, religious righteousness, and even guilt), to thoughts (think of obsessions), to activities (workaholism, gambling, compulsive exercising and sexual behavior, spending and hoarding), to being in control, and even to reenactments of victimization and other trauma.

Any of these activities that lead to "life-damaging consequences" and loss of control qualifies as an addiction or compulsion, according to addictions expert John Bradshaw. He defines a "life-damaging consequence" as one that threatens one's health, safety, or livelihood, one's relationships with other people, or the health and safety of others. And, he says, the loss of control is one of the bitter ironies of the addictive/compulsive dilemma. When we try to control our addictions and compulsions, we have to face our underlying shame.

If you find yourself frequently tired, anxious, or angry, if you can't seem to connect to the people you want to be close to, if you feel you are on a treadmill and can't get off, chances are there is some compulsive or addictive process at work. We often rationalize these activities as necessary, fun, or "no big deal," but the truth is they leave us emotionally hungry and interfere with the intimacy that could truly satisfy us if we weren't so darned scared of it.

When addictions and compulsions occur in people who have a predominantly narcissistic style or character structure, which is more often the case than not, the behavior is likely to be especially entrenched and well-defended. The unhealthy Narcissist sees these behaviors as fundamentally beneficial, nondestructive, and in any event necessary to his or her emotional survival. Any confrontation to the contrary is likely to evoke shame and its defenses of denial and/or rage. Otto Kernberg, who gave us much of what we know about pathological narcissism, believes the addictive potential in narcissistic personality structures is maximal, and the prognosis for treatment is much worse than for other types of personality disorder or in people who have fewer personality defects. What that means for you if you are dealing with an addictive or compulsive Narcissist in your life, whether that person is a sports junkie, a shopaholic, a sex fiend, a religious nut, a control freak, or actually chemically dependent, is that you might as well beat your head against the wall as try to change them. If you want relief, you're going to have to change *you*.

Strategy One: Know Yourself

People who are drawn to and remain in relationships with addicted and compulsive others are called co-dependents, and they usually have their own not-so-healthy reasons for needing to control or take care of those who are out of control. Co-dependency is also an addiction, and it even has its own 12-step program, CoDA, or Co-Dependents Anonymous. The fourth step of any 12-step program is to make a Personal Inventory, which means to take stock of one's own destructive behavior and how it has damaged oneself and others. This can be enormously revealing and empowering.

If you have a parent, spouse, or other significant person in your life who is an addictive or compulsive Narcissist, chances are you have developed your own compulsions or addictions for dealing with the stress of this relationship. Maybe you need a glass or two of wine in the evening to face this person over dinner. Maybe you need a little grass to make love. Maybe you crave chocolate, or potato chips, or ice cream and have trouble controlling your weight. Maybe you immerse yourself in the practice of your religion in order to convert the pain and emptiness of your life into something with transcendent meaning. Maybe you have to have a new pair of shoes for every social occasion. Maybe you can't stop collecting "toys"—electronic equipment, sporting goods, furniture, cars, art, whatever you do for a hobby. Maybe you read, or sew, or clean compulsively, to distract yourself from your unsatisfying life. Maybe you are always on the lookout for the next thrill, or the next relationship, that can get you "high." Maybe you run a tab at Starbucks or keep the tobacco industry in business. You don't have to be an alcoholic or a drug addict, an anorexic or a bulimic, a pathological gambler or a Type-A workaholic to have a problem with compulsion. Anything that you do to alter your mood that keeps you from addressing underlying problems could be hurting you—or someone you love—more than it is helping.

What do you do to make bad feelings go away? Could you stop any of these behaviors if you knew they were hurting your child, your spouse, your best friend? What if the one being hurt was you? Is there something going on in your life that you avoid or distract yourself from because it feels too overwhelming or unsolvable? Are things out of control?

Strategy Two: Embrace Reality

It is one thing to recognize a problem, another to actually do something about it. That requires vigilance, discipline, and staying in touch with reality. The normal human tendency is to let things slide, but conversely, even vigilance and discipline can become compulsive. To become compulsive about our compulsions is to invite more shame into our lives. What we need is a realistic assessment of our circumstances and a realistic plan of action. If you are addicted to drugs, alcohol, or nicotine, you will sooner or later have to face letting go of that substance, one day at a time. But in most other types of addiction and compulsion, it is a matter of establishing balance. When you practice living a balanced life, it feels different, and you may very well need a plan for handling the feelings that come up. When you stop altering your moods, you have to face the feelings that you have avoided. How well you work through those feelings will have everything to do with whether you will be able to live a life free of addictions and compulsions. That is reality.

Many people find that they cannot work through these feelings on their own. In addition to professional help, there are many self-help groups and 12-Step programs that focus on all kinds of problems. No matter where you live, chances are good that there are resources close at hand. You don't have to make a commitment just to check these out, and to do so could be a powerful first step toward a healthier, more comfortable and balanced life.

Strategy Three: Set Boundaries

Recovering from your own addictions and compulsions, especially if they have developed in relationship to someone else who is also addictive, compulsive, and narcissistic, means separating yourself from that person and his or her influences. To really get healthy, you may have to let go of some relationships or radically restructure others, such as a marriage or family tie. In order to change the way you dance with someone, you may have to sit out a few sets. The timeout gives you perspective on the ways you get hooked into the addictive/compulsive tango.

Setting boundaries with the addictive/compulsive Narcissist might include any of the following:

- refusing to use or abuse substances at the urging of the Narcissist, or to accompany that person to a place where such substances will be used or abused;

- saying no to sexual activities that the Narcissist wants but which make you uncomfortable;

- refusing to lend money to the Narcissist for the pursuit of his or her addiction/compulsion;

- avoiding rescuing the Narcissist from the consequences of his or her addictive/compulsive behavior;

- declining to participate excessively in any activity that is of little or no value to you when the sole purpose of your participation is to meet the Narcissist's demands;

- standing up to or otherwise protecting yourself from abusive treatment that results from the Narcissist's addiction or compulsion;

- insisting on protection for yourself and dependent others from dangers associated with the Narcissist's addictions

    or compulsions, and making sure those protections are
    enforced;

- insisting on time and resources for yourself to pursue
  your own interests, regardless of objections from the Narcissist;

- refusing to go along with anything when you feel intimidated, manipulated, or exploited, or because the Narcissist might get angry or petulant if you don't give in to his
  or her demands.

If saying no and standing up to an addictive/compulsive Narcissist
feels too scary or overwhelming, you might want to consider if it is in
your best interests to continue in this relationship. If you can't get out
on your own, get help.

Strategy Four: Cultivate Reciprocal Relationships

The ironic thing about relationships where addictions and compulsions are prominent is that they usually are reciprocal—in unhealthy
ways. The quid pro quo isn't always apparent even to the partici-
pants, but you usually don't have to look very deeply to find it. "Hidden agendas"—those tacit expectations that cause all sorts of
problems when someone misses or misinterprets an indirect cue or
unilaterally changes an unspoken "rule"—are the glue that holds two
compulsive people together. Feed or tolerate my addiction/compul-
sion that we agree not to openly acknowledge, and I'll feed, tolerate,
and keep quiet about yours.

    The sad thing about such relationships, however, is that there is al-
most never any real intimacy, or when there is, it can't be sustained
because somebody, usually two somebodies, become(s) a little too uneasy about keeping up the connection. Intimacy is the cure for addictive and compulsive relationships and behaviors, but if you can't
stand the heat, you're probably going to stay out of the kitchen where
healthy reciprocal relationships are lovingly prepared and relished.

16

Narcissists in Love: The Fusion Delusion

NARCISSISTS ARE PEOPLE WHO never learned to make it on their own. Except for their fantasies of perfection, envy of others who have what they lack, and unacknowledged fears of humiliation, they are empty on the inside. They have no real Self to bring to a relationship with another person, but they desperately need someone else to join them in their emptiness and help them maintain emotional equilibrium. The ideal candidate is someone willing to become an extension of the Narcissist's fragile ego, to serve as an object of admiration, contempt, or often enough both. The sign over their door ought to read: Abandon Self All Ye Who Enter Here.

The Fusion Delusion

In a healthy passionate relationship, two people have as much regard for each other's separate existence as they do for their own. They surrender themselves in moments of union and feel expanded rather than diminished by the tumble into love. As the boundaries of Self melt away, they merge with someone who represents their heart's desire and transcend the existential aloneness that comes with psychological autonomy. They move in and out of such moments with ease, knowing that their separateness only enhances their union, and vice versa. They admire each other's real attributes and can tolerate their loved one's shortcomings without becoming ashamed or enraged.

How different this is from the Fusion Delusion that passes for love among the narcissistically impaired. When two such lovers connect, the goal for one—and often enough for the other as well—is complete and total merger, the obliteration of one partner's autonomy in the service of the other's narcissism. In a psychological sense, there cease to be two separate people in this mutation of love. The fusion of two impoverished souls engaged in a dance of power suggests that there are narcissistic processes at work in both.

The more flagrantly narcissistic partner is usually the one whose entitlement, grandiosity, arrogance, admiration-seeking, lack of empathy, or exploitation are most obvious to outside observers. This is often the more charismatic of the two, the one who draws attention, whether positive or negative. It is generally not difficult to discern that it is this person's ego that is the dominant force in the relationship, the one that will eclipse and subsume the other. The resulting "undifferentiated ego mass" appears to be owned and controlled by the dominant partner. On the other side of this equation is a partner who tolerates or may even welcome being taken over in this way.

The person who submits to the tyranny of a Narcissist often appears to be an enigma. Why would anyone choose, repeatedly and perpetually, to offer him- or herself as fuel for another's consuming need for inflation, and at such a price? Why would someone sacrifice Self so completely for "love"?

The nickel answer to this question is that he or she has been programmed to self-effacement and self-abasement by earlier life experi-

ences. Perhaps he had a narcissistic parent and learned to feel worthy only when meeting that person's needs. Subsequent relationships that recreate the original dynamics seem to offer the possibility of a different outcome. "This time I will be loved for myself," he hopes. But it's not in the cards.

A somewhat more sophisticated explanation is that in having learned to submit, she has figured out how to exert some power in an otherwise powerless situation, providing a fleeting sense of strength and control. Often, such morsels suffice for survival of the soul. And in extreme cases when someone has been so abused that self-hatred is great, there may even be a sort of relief in giving oneself over to someone perceived as more worthy.

Even healthy people are drawn to the merger aspects of passionate love, but they are able both to transcend boundaries and to maintain them. Their healthy narcissism leads them to admire someone who reflects their own ideals, to form attachments to others in their entirety and separateness, and to maintain a love relationship over an extended period of time—something that the Narcissist can accomplish only amid great conflict. There is an element of altruism in healthy love that mingles self-centeredness with self-sacrifice and concern for the loved one's feelings and well-being, and sexual contact is more than a search for pleasure—it is also an expression of gratitude for the partner's love.

For Narcissists, however, fulfillment comes from having conquered or won the love object, annihilating that person's separateness and replacing it with a fantasy "twinship." They seek someone who will reflect back their importance and who can also be the receptacle for their off-loaded shame and envy. The partner is merely a means for the Narcissist to negotiate different parts of himself, amplifying his assets and ridding himself of defects.

There are only two kinds of people of any use to Narcissists: those who can pump them up and those whom they can put down. The ones who can pump them up may do so either by admiring them or

by sharing their own special attributes so the Narcissist can bask in their reflected glow. The ones whom they can put down allow Narcissists either to off-load shame via projection or to feel superior by comparison. The love objects of Narcissists often serve both functions. If you're hooked on a Narcissist, prepare to tolerate regular doses of contempt while offering unending admiration, which the Narcissist is far more interested in than your love.

While it's normal to idealize those we love, to the Narcissist, his own self-image requires that other people also see the love object in an idealized way. Toward that end, he must select someone who is beautiful, intelligent, accomplished, or otherwise widely recognized as exceptional. The Narcissist hopes to commandeer those admirable qualities that he or she lacks, acquiring "gilt" by association.

Smothering Heights: The Tale of Dennis and Christina

Of all the facets of his career as a professor of English literature, Dennis most enjoyed the lecture. He liked to arrive late so he could make an entrance, and he relished that moment just before his students began taking notes when all eyes were on him.

It was at a moment such as this when he had first noticed Christina, and her large pale eyes and smooth complexion had reminded him of the heroines in the books he admired. Her beauty excited something primal within him, and it wasn't long before he resolved to win her love.

He began by wooing her surreptitiously with his words. She became his audience of one, the others fading into background as he courted her secretly, willing her to be stirred by his covert passion and to betray some yearning of her own. In time, she began to respond to him, just as he wished.

By spring they were lovers, and possessing her was everything he had imagined it would be. She was perfection, and, he was convinced, completely and totally his. Being able to call her his own made him feel as if he, too, was a character in a romantic novel.

She moved in with him after graduation, and although she had a degree in economics, that was of no consequence in the future he envisioned for

them together. He planned that they would marry when he got tenure, and then they would have a child while on sabbatical in England. She would be the inspiration and the sounding-board for the novel he planned to write and would charm his friends at faculty gatherings and the small dinner parties that he would host to showcase their perfect love. With Christina, he felt himself to be the envy of every man in the English department.

Although Narcissists intend for others to envy them their conquests, they are unaware of how envious they themselves feel of the ones who become their love objects. Narcissists are essentially competitive people, and the very qualities that attract them at the outset of a relationship in time begin to make them feel inferior by comparison. The person who seemed so capable of feeding their hunger for admiration later becomes a threat, and they need to tear that person down in order to build themselves back up. Whatever Narcissists admire in a loved one also diminishes them and therefore must be detroyed. Envy leads to contempt and contempt to destruction, leaving Narcissists frustrated and empty in their pursuit of perfection.

Envy, like shame, is a sordid emotion that Narcissists can't tolerate. Instead of admitting to themselves that they're envious, they get rid of the bad feelings by making them belong to someone else. By a trick of mind called *projection,* the envied person becomes the one who harbors these unacceptable thoughts, and the Narcissist remains admirable in his or her own eyes as well as the eyes of the world. By this same mechanism, Narcissists also attribute their own destructive urges to other people and are terrified of the real or imagined envy that surrounds them. These distortions make real intimacy impossible.

For Narcissists, all relationships are about exploitation, and it's eat or be eaten. The idea of making themselves vulnerable is no more than an invitation to be used. When someone becomes dependent on them, they feel as if they're being taken advantage of, and fear of being exploited also makes them deny their own dependency. Ordinary reciprocity feels to them as if they're being invaded and used, so they insist on relationships in which they always maintain the upper hand.

Christina's Story

It was my senior year, and I was pretty saturated with economics, thought I would take an elective completely outside of my major. Some of my friends had told me about this English professor who made the classics come alive. It sounded like fun and a good way to finish up my undergraduate studies, a chance to get a little culture before going on for my MBA.

But what happened took me completely by surprise. Dennis was just mesmerizing. Sitting in his class, I felt practically spellbound, as if I was the only person in this big lecture hall, like he was talking just to me. Then at some point I realized that he was talking to me in some special way. I started hanging around after class on any pretext I could think of, and before long, I was madly in love with him. I had had a couple of boyfriends, but this was a man, ten years older than me. Usually, I tried to keep my relationships casual because I didn't want anything to interfere with my education, and I had a career mapped out for myself that would keep me in school for a long time. But all that went out the window when I fell in love with Dennis.

In the spring, I went through the motions of applying to graduate programs, but I was pretty distracted. Whenever I tried to talk to Dennis about my career plans, he would kind of fade out. At first I thought maybe he was just sad about the prospect of our being separated and couldn't talk about it. It actually made me feel closer to him to think that he cared that much. I figured I'd wait and see what happened and we'd deal with it when the time came.

After graduation, I moved in with him, and I'd been living there about a month when I found out I'd been accepted at NYU. I was so excited and I thought Dennis would be happy for me, too, but he got really cold, and I'll never forget what he said to me. "Christina, if you turn your back on my love, you will never know the happiness you've missed. No one will ever love you the way I do." That was it. There was no discussion, no compro-

mise. He made me choose. I gave it a lot of thought—I really did—and I decided he was right. No career could be worth the love we had.

From that point on, he pretty much took charge of my life, and I just allowed myself to be swept along. When things go according to his plans, it's like magic and we're so happy. But if something doesn't work out the way he wants it to, it's a completely different story. He doesn't just get disappointed like other people, it's like he's really angry. And he can stay that way for days, unless I can figure out how to cheer him up. Ever since our son came along, that's been harder and harder to do. Byron was born with a cleft palate, and sometimes I think Dennis blames me. I know it sounds crazy—he adores me!—but sometimes I get this feeling that Dennis looks down on me, like maybe I'm intellectually inferior or something. Maybe I should have gone to graduate school after all, so he could still respect me. Sometimes I just feel so confused.

In Christina, Dennis found the perfect mate who perfectly mirrored his grandiosity and omnipotence and completely folded herself into him. Having won her love, his inflation was at first boundless. Love such as Dennis's is like a drug, a perpetual high that insulates the lover from self-doubt and awareness of personal limits or shortcomings. But to maintain the intoxication, he must be able to control his most prized possession.

The means by which the Narcissist controls the loved one are many and varied, a function of individual style, circumstances, and opportunity. They can be as sweetly beguiling as flattery and professions of love, as maddening as the carrot that dangles just beyond reach, as manipulative as the polar opposites of subservience and moral superiority, or as intimidating as a volcano about to explode. The goal is to maintain the obliteration of the loved one's separateness, the Fusion Delusion.

It is important to Narcissists to choose those who will look up to them, recognize their special qualities, and make them feel important. While we all want to be valued by those we love, the Narcissist really needs the loved one to be a constant mirror of his or her worth. Any of us might feel disappointed, hurt, or even angry when those we love ignore or criticize us, but the Narcissist becomes enraged when the pipeline for inflation is ruptured. The loved one is not allowed to have or express feelings or opinions that contradict the needs of the Narcissist.

Often the Narcissist selects a love object who is in some way deficient or less powerful, someone who can be easily manipulated or controlled. This is tricky, however. If this person becomes too much of a doormat, too degraded or flawed in the eyes of the Narcissist, idealization may be compromised. The Narcissist usually solves this problem by splitting good and bad perceptions of the love object so that the good can be preserved in some way and the bad remains walled off in a compartment that can be opened or closed at will. This is very much like the primitive way in which very young children are unable to see others as complex entities with both good and bad qualities. At any given moment, someone is either all good or all bad. And the Narcissist's perception of the love object can change in an instant.

Because of this inability to hold an image of the love object as both good *and* bad, the Narcissist will "forget," overlook, or dismiss any of his or her own behavior that demeans this person, all the while expecting the love object to live up to idealized expectations, particularly in public and regardless of how much humiliation the Narcissist has inflicted. If the Narcissist can't mobilize enough fantasy or denial to sustain the necessary idealization, the erstwhile love object may be discarded in favor of someone who is less tarnished. It is hard to continue to hold in high regard someone who has been made a slave, even if that person is one's own slave.

Don Juans and Ice Queens

Narcissists are ultimately the worst lovers, with a full range of every sexual dysfunction imaginable and a tendency to use their partners selfishly and without guilt. Heterosexual and bisexual narcissistic men harbor a deep envy of women and fear being rejected and ridiculed by them. They tend to objectify their partners either as idealized but desexualized objects (the "pure" mother, or madonna), or those who can be freely enjoyed without love or admiration (the "soiled" mother, or whore). Conversely, they may also develop tender feelings for women who turn them off sexually. Many are Don Juans of one flavor or another, some aggressive, some merely compulsive, some rather childlike. The aggressive Don Juan is the guy who gets his jollies from frustrating or humiliating a woman he's seduced, and he seems almost relieved when he dumps her after a brief tryst. The more compulsive Don Juan is just plowing through the female population looking for the one woman who won't disappoint him. Then there's the infantile Don Juan, an effeminate man-child who succeeds with women precisely because he lacks those masculine qualities that some women find threatening.

Narcissistic women tend to be cold and calculating, with considerable hostility toward both men and women. They will use a partner as long as the hapless lover allows it, but if that lover musters some self-respect and finally bolts, they may be angry and spiteful but will never pine away or feel guilty. The more promiscuous among them see a prince in every new admirer, only to lose interest when he turns out to be a frog after all.

Rockets for Laura

Laura floats through the door and throws herself on the couch, surrendering to the well-worn cushions. "I think I'm in love!" she announces dreamily, swooning as she kicks off her shoes. "Do tell," says her roommate Beth, "and who would be the Dupe du Jour?"

"His name is David," Laura replies, ignoring the verbal dart. "We've been eying each other at Starbuck's for over a week, and today he finally made the move. He bought me a double latte, and we've been talking for hours. You wouldn't believe how much we have in common! He's a film

student at USC—his uncle is a producer!—and he's doing this project, David is, on—oh, what's his name? that guy who's running for city council from West Hollywood? Anyway, I told him about how I worked on the mayor's campaign and what politics is like on the inside. And then it turns out he goes rock climbing on weekends, he's hooked on Thai food, and— get this!—he has not one but two Labrador retrievers! I mean, could we possibly have anything more in common? Oh, and did I mention, he has Leo DiCaprio's mouth, and he thinks I look like Neve Campbell? This is just too perfect!

Roll 'em, thinks Beth, who has seen this movie about five times now in the two years she has been sharing an apartment with Laura. Act One always plays like this: Laura comes home on Cloud Nine, certain she has met the Love of Her Life. In Act Two, Beth gets to meet The Guy, who has a few things going for him but is hardly the god Laura has portrayed him to be. The plot features a romance that takes off like a rocket, peaks somewhere in the ozone, and then, in Act Three, comes crashing back to Earth. The time frame usually spans several months, but sometimes it's all over in a matter of weeks. The weirdest part of the story is that Laura always walks away from the crash without a scratch. Whatever disappointment she feels can usually be salved with a trip to the mall and a night on the town, where she can strut her stuff before the local swains. Beth is beginning to get the picture that, when it comes to love, Laura's more interested in the launch than the journey—and her companion is just along for the ride.

Less adventuresome narcissistic women than Laura tend to settle into stable relationships with partners they consider to be "the very best." Others may be fixated on unavailable love objects whose very remoteness permits them to remain hermetically sealed in their perfection, all the better to protect the Narcissist from the risk of being devalued in a real relationship. Sometimes they attach themselves to extremely narcissistic and accomplished partners, believing themselves to be the inspiration for the partner's greatness or even ending up running that person's life.

Some of these arrangements involve an exhibitionistic Narcissist and a partner who is "in the closet." The closet Narcissist is an unassuming type who has her feelers out for someone she can idealize. She needs to put the love object on a pedestal in order to hold herself together, because if her partner is wonderful and she can have him, then all the insecurities inside her will go away. In the Narcissist–closet Narcissist couple, it is actually the latter who is in control, feeding the grandiosity of the love object in order to inflate herself via osmosis. These relationships can be quite successful, as long as the idealizations and illusions can be sustained. But when unpleasant reality intrudes, love implodes.

Complementarity: The Love of Justin and Luisa

They met while Justin was still a promising young concert violinist and Luisa was studying merchandising at the local junior college. He admired her beauty and gentle demeanor, she the promise he represented of one day escaping a mundane blue-collar existence. Until she met him, all of Luisa's hopes were pinned on becoming a buyer in a high-class department store. Now she saw her destiny in him—he would travel and become famous, and she would devote her life to helping him make his dreams come true. She was convinced that he was exceptional, and from the moment she met him, her world became larger and more meaningful.

Justin had never known anyone quite like Luisa. There had been many women in his life, but each had become tiresome after a time. They had always turned out to be selfish and demanding, not understanding of his goals and the delicate temperament of a gifted musician.

In Justin's eyes, Luisa was really quite enchanting. He loved her lustrous dark hair and delicate hands and the way she laughed at his jokes. She was one of the few women he had ever encountered who consistently "got" his humor. It was as if they shared one mind. And she loved his music. She would beg him to play for her and was delighted with his compositions. She believed he could do anything, and since she had come into his life, he, too, felt his star was rising.

So sure was Justin of his future that he grew intolerant of any career frustration that seemed to challenge his sense of superiority. His peers in the orchestra found him arrogant and increasingly difficult to get along with. Although he was younger than most of the others, he seemed to expect them to recognize that he was special. When the first chair became vacant and was offered to someone else, he walked out of rehearsal. He was summarily fired.

Luisa was as mystified as Justin was outraged, but she was certain that better things were in store for him as a solo performer of his own compositions. She soothed and comforted him endlessly, urging him to look at this turn of events as an opportunity to redirect his career. She could support them while he made the magic happen. She knew it wouldn't be long.

Weeks passed, and then months, as Justin nursed his deeply wounded pride and tried half-heartedly to resurrect his star. He brooded, he drank, he slept late, and occasionally he made phone calls to agents or picked up his abandoned violin. Luisa tried to encourage him, but her patience began to falter and she could feel the disillusionment creeping in. Her ministrations became mechanical, but Justin never noticed.

One day, alone in their apartment, Justin stumbled across Luisa's diary and, without hesitation, he began to thumb through its contents. He was shocked by what he read. Luisa—his Luisa!—had poured out her heart . . . about another man! She was in love, or so it seemed, with someone whom she described as her soulmate. The relationship had been going on for some time, and he was on the verge of losing her. Impossible!

From that day forward, Justin could not look at Luisa in the same way. She had fallen from the pedestal he had erected for her, smashed to the ground, and like Humpty-Dumpty, she couldn't be put back together again. When he confronted her, she tried to reassure him, but clearly the light had gone out of her eyes, too. It was over, and, Justin thought ruefully, she was just like the rest after all.

Luisa, for her part, was left feeling strangely flat. She tried to connect with her feelings. Well, there was resentment toward Justin for letting her down and guilt about her longings for another man, but when all was said and done, Luisa mostly just felt empty. Surely there was more to love than this. Next time, she vowed, she would have to set her sights higher.

The narcissistic love match is inherently unstable. Any intrusion of reality can destabilize the relationship, leading to chronic or intermittent conflict, misery, trips to the couple counselor, or dramatic ruptures that bring the union to an end.

When the Narcissist can find support outside the relationship—career, family, friends, or other interests—that keep him or her feeling pumped up, the pressure on the partner may be minimal. But frustrations at work, job loss or retirement, disruptions in other needed relationships, and losses in status or rewards from other pipelines usually lead to more demands on the partner to pick up the slack.

It is the nature of human beings to seek more satisfying solutions to life's challenges over time and to strive toward a fully realized evolution of Self. Even a seed of emotional health wants to grow. Just as primary narcissism is a transient state in early childhood, so may narcissistic relationships be way stations on our journey to mature love. But sometimes the hard part is figuring out if, when, and how to move on.

Guidelines for Survival: When You Are in Love with a Narcissist

What draws us into love relationships with Narcissists? For one thing, they really are "special," although not always in the ways they would like to be. Their tendency to pursue idealized fantasies can spin a magic web around mundane reality, appealing to your need for glamour and excitement. And when their hunger for admiration makes them want to please *you,* it can feel like real love. In some cases, their grandiosity may seem to offer something that is missing from your life. Even their arrogance can be appealing if your self-esteem is a little shaky and you're easily impressed with someone who seems so confident. And to be the love choice of such a celestial body—ooh-la-la!—can be quite intoxicating, at least for a while.

Passionate love, with its obsessions, longings for merger, attendant feelings of grandiosity and omnipotence, and deep ties to our primitive past, is so full of narcissistic elements that it is often difficult to distinguish what is deliriously normal from what is essentially unhealthy. If my beloved doesn't always understand me or put my needs first, does that mean he's unempathic or she's selfish? If I'm expected to do things I don't particularly want to do from time to time, does that mean I'm being abused or exploited? Is it wrong to want to be in control? No, no, and no. So how do I know if my love relationship is healthy or narcissistic?

The core element of a relationship that is fundamentally narcissistic is the Fusion Delusion, that fantasy that we are, or should be, completely and forever One. Separateness is a threat. Envy lurks around every corner. Boundaries are not respected because they don't exist to begin with. A power imbalance, with domination on one side and submission on the other, is common, although the partners may swap roles from time to time. This does not make the relationship reciprocal, because genuine mutuality is also nonexistent. If any of this seems uncomfortably familiar, let's see how the Survival Strategies apply when you're in love.

Strategy One: Know Yourself

Our earliest experiences of loving and being loved replay throughout our lives, and love's longings may beckon us all to revisit those toddler days of union with a wonderful and powerful Mother. Each of the developmental dramas in the Birth of Me—symbiosis, practicing, and rapprochement—shape our perceptions of Self and others in ways that determine who and how we love. If we were securely attached in childhood to someone who nurtured our autonomy, we will choose a partner who does the same and will not need fantasy to sustain love. But if our autonomy was thwarted, stranding us on the outskirts of separation-individuation, we may re-enact the dynamics of fusion, grandiosity, and omnipotence with others whose personal boundaries are similarly blurred.

For some of us, the period of symbiosis—when we first became psychologically merged with Mother—was anything but blissful. If she was nonresponsive during this stage, we may find ourselves longing for love without really expecting that it will ever come. If, on the other hand, she was overly intrusive, we may habitually defend our boundaries from any and all invaders, including the well-intentioned. When we come from such "misattuned" backgrounds, to love is to be unfulfilled, and to let love in is to invite engulfment and annihilation. Only fantasy love, love with built-in obstacles, or unrequited love may seem safe enough. The Narcissist may seem like a good match for our low expectations.

If you grew up in a family in which one or both parents were Narcissists, chances are good that you are vulnerable to love relationships that have a distinctly narcissistic flavor. Here are some of the ways this legacy might affect you now:

- You fall in love quickly or frequently, or conversely, you are afraid to let someone get close for fear that you will be exploited or rejected.

- Only "perfect love" seems safe or exciting enough, or, at the other end of the spectrum, you usually pick inappropriate or unavailable partners.

- After you've known them awhile and the first blush of romance fades, loved ones seem to reveal flaws or become difficult.

- You've never been in love and can't imagine what it would be like, or the flip side, you can never seem to get enough love from someone you care about.

- You have trouble giving, or taking, in an intimate relationship.

- You need to idealize, or devalue, a loved one in order to feel good about yourself.

- You have trouble apologizing to your loved one, or just the opposite, you take responsibility for everything unpleasant that happens between you.

- You often feel hurt, or disappointed, in love.

Remember, no one had a perfect childhood, and we all experience conflict in close relationships from time to time. But if you feel you tend to lose yourself in an intimate relationship or have difficulty recognizing someone else's needs and rights, if you are threatened or confused about boundaries, you will need to try to figure out what is going on in you and in the relationship that may be a re-enactment of unhealthy narcissism. If possible, try to engage your partner in an exploration of the problems. The openness to explore this together is a good sign. One of the best ways to recover from the impact of unhealthy narcissism is to create a healthy love relationship in the present. This begins with respectful, empathic communication and an understanding of each other's "buttons."

Strategy Two: Embrace Reality

Your accurate assessment of your own strengths and weaknesses, as well as those of your partner and of the relationship, is your best tool in managing unhealthy narcissism. You will have to look past any need you may have for perfection, as well as whatever distortions your partner contributes to making things unreal. This can be painful and difficult, because it involves disengaging from the Fusion Delusion—to whatever extent this has been a part of your relationship. You are actually recreating that developmental step from early childhood in which you begin to see yourself and the object of your affection as having both good and bad qualities, in other words, being whole, complex, and ultimately imperfect. To be able to do this without overwhelming rage or shame is a good sign.

Many people fear the loss of idealization in a love relationship. They think they won't be able to keep love alive without a sense of mystery based on hiding flaws, denying defects, and obscuring unpleasant truths. They need to create and maintain a fantasy world that protects their love from harsh reality. If this is your theory of love, it will take a great deal of courage to test that hypothesis. What you stand to gain is the freedom to be yourself and to be loved for who you really are, warts and all. Healthy lovers are able to idealize their loved one's unique real attributes with full awareness of their equally real shortcomings. They don't expect perfection, perfect attunement to their needs, or perfect compliance with their wishes. Instead, they relish the ways they are challenged and enriched by interaction with someone truly separate.

Strategy Three: Set Boundaries

Good self-boundaries are a sign of separateness and emotional strength. Evaluate the health of your love relationship by considering the following boundary issues and how you and your partner negotiate any differences you may have:

- How do you handle separate time, separate friends, and separate interests?

- How do you make decisions about how to use your leisure time?

- Is there privacy within the relationship, or do you open each other's mail; go through each other's purse, wallet, or pockets without asking; eavesdrop on each other's phone conversations or read each other's e-mail?

- Can you have your own thoughts, feelings, or other personal experiences without having to explain or describe them to your partner unless you want to?

- Are you able to disagree without feeling wounded or angry?

- What has happened when—or what do you think would happen if—you insisted on creating or enforcing such boundaries? Are you able to ask without fear of an angry or shaming response, or some kind or retaliation? Would your partner listen and respond with respect?

All couples must negotiate boundaries that are comfortable for both partners. How you resolve your differences—with respect and accommodation, or with manipulation and anger—can be a measure of the unhealthy narcissism in your relationship. If boundary conflicts are a source of discomfort, consider whether there are narcissistic forces at work.

Some unhealthy relationships have boundaries that are too rigid. Two people coexist in their own separate worlds without ever having moments of merger, much less a continuing sense of deep connection. Can you get your partner's attention when you really need to? Would each of you be willing to make a sacrifice for the other's well-being? Is your sexual relationship satisfying, or is it wooden and perfunctory? Do you often feel alone while with this person? When two very self-absorbed people find themselves in a relationship of convenience, the "love" may be of the self-aggrandizing variety, an attachment that confers, for example, wealth or social advantage and the illusion of specialness. In this case, there is no Fusion Delusion but rather a deep resistance to becoming vulnerable and surrendering to the transcendent experience of passionate love.

Strategy Four: Cultivate Reciprocal Relationships

The hallmark of mature love is reciprocity, in which two people have as much regard for each other as they do for themselves. The Narcissist, in contrast, does not love in any mature, reciprocal, or nurturant sense of the word. It is all about Me. In narcissistic love, one person's Self is submerged in the service of propping up another's fragile ego. Rather than the self-transcendence of two, there is only the self-inflation of one.

Reciprocity is about give and take. Narcissists may think of themselves as givers, but they only give what they want. This is selfish giving, without recognition of what others want or need. It's really more a convoluted form of taking, self-deluded and self-inflating. If someone consistently experiences another's real longing as a demand or an imposition and responds with annoyance, distancing, or contempt, there is no reciprocity. Conversely, those who are unsure of their own worth and uncomfortable with asking or taking make their own complementary contribution to lopsided narcissistic love. Reciprocity requires self-esteem on both sides of the equation.

True reciprocity also requires mutual trust. If you are having trouble with this aspect of an intimate relationship, see if you can let down your guard with a friend or family member, someone with whom you feel safe. Once you know what it feels like to be both a giver and a receiver, you may be able to translate that experience to a romantic relationship. To be successful, however, you will need to choose a partner who is not a Narcissist. Lose your heart to love, but keep your Self for you.

17

Narcissists at Work:
The Abuse of Power

THE MOST SUCCESSFUL NARCISSISTS always command a piece of
turf, whether it be a large corporation, a small department, a congre-
gation—anything, really, from a family to a whole country. The
ranks of the wealthy and the famous are replete with narcissistic
characters, but so are small businesses and job environments of every
size and ilk. Power is the perfect antidote for shame, and the Narcissist sees power as his due. There is no internal struggle between self-
interest and empathy for others to block his path, so only a lack of
gifts or ambition will limit him. The Narcissist, however, must be
ever wary of envious rivals and protective of his turf. Watch him and
see how he maintains control, not only of his sphere of influence but
also over the specters of powerlessness, humiliation, envy, and void
that haunt him from within. If you play in his game, know what you
are up against.

Eight Characteristics of the Narcissist in Power

To rise to the top of an organization, to build a business, to win an election, to compete favorably in any market requires healthy narcissism, the confidence to activate one's talents and skills in a sustained way toward an identified goal, despite setbacks and obstacles. In the absence of healthy narcissism, however, unhealthy narcissism will often do quite nicely. But when the person at the helm is an emotional toddler, the work environment can become toxic. Fear, mistrust, and exhaustion make life miserable for everyone, interfering with both morale and productivity. Think about the problems you've experienced on a job. Who has had the power and how has it been exercised? How have you been affected? If you've felt stressed, angry, or overwhelmed, ask yourself if any of the following applies to the person or people in charge.

1. Poor Interpersonal Boundaries

Equilibrium for Narcissists is a state of fusion with others who have something they need. Whether the Narcissist deliberately sets out to undermine your autonomy or just ignores your separate existence, that predisposition to fusion means that you will not only be expected to do what the Narcissist wants but also to know what that is, to want it yourself, and—this is important—to be able to produce it. It is as if you must live inside the Narcissist's head, share her thoughts and feelings, and be able to perform things that even she isn't able to do. Anything less is an affront to her narcissistic sense of entitlement and need for perfect mirroring.

If the Narcissist wants you for something, you become an extension of her Self, like an extra arm on her body. She may flatter you, offer you rewards, or otherwise try to seduce you to get you into her web. If she already has power over you, she may shame or manipulate you to keep you under her thumb. Her goal is to annihilate the boundaries between you, to own you, as it were. Separateness will be viewed as a threat, and you will experience repeated violations of your personal boundaries. These are the people who will tell you that the workplace is "like a family" and will want to know the details of your personal life, your health, your outside relationships. Narcissism is often the core pathology of the person who makes inappropriate sexual advances toward a subordinate, who carries on office affairs, or who encourages "dual relationships," such as the supervisor who asks a file clerk to baby-sit for her children on the weekend. Personal boundaries are seen as an obstacle to complete control and are routinely violated. When you become aware of poor interpersonal boundaries, you are in the presence of a real Narcissist. Be careful.

Belinda's Story

Belinda, a bright and attractive young woman employed at a small advertising firm, presented for therapy with a rather unusual complaint: Her bosses had rated her "nonassertive" on a performance evaluation and, out of "concern for her emotional well-being," had recommended that she seek psychotherapy. "We really like you," they told her, "but we're worried that your lack of assertiveness will interfere with your ability to service your accounts." They had no hard evidence that this was in fact the case; on the contrary, Belinda's thoroughness and attention to others' needs had made her very popular with her customers. Something just didn't add up.

Nevertheless, Belinda was devastated by her bosses' suggestion that her composed demeanor and carefully chosen words were somehow evidence of a personal defect severe enough to warrant treatment. By the time she reached the therapist's office, she was wracked with self-doubt and had been experiencing sleep and appetite problems, signs that she was becoming depressed.

Belinda appeared to have no trouble articulating her feelings in acceptable ways, and there was little in her history that would contribute to her developing the low self-esteem that usually underlies problems with assertiveness. The eldest of three children in a close, intact family, she had always been an achiever, and it was clear that she felt good about herself and her accomplishments. Her life had not been idyllic by any means, and she had made some mistakes in her younger years, but on the whole, she was functioning like a healthy, normal adult. Her biggest problem was her job.

The small firm where Belinda worked was a model of bad boundaries. The man and woman who co-owned the business ran it like a Mom-and-Pop store. The man's sister was one of the seven employees, and her best friend, also an employee, was dating the female boss's ex-husband. Alliances were constantly shifting as sibling rivalries, volatile friendships, and the detritus of divorce made it unsafe to trust anyone. The bosses liked to see themselves as benevolent parents, but in fact they were often unreasonable tyrants, prone to tantrums and sullenness when things didn't go their way or they had taken on more business than they could handle. Belinda's quite natural, not to mention healthy, reaction was to retreat into a protective shell of professionalism that was seen as an affront to the company's "family" image of itself. Belinda was expected to socialize after hours with her colleagues and was frequently asked probing questions about her medical appointments and her relationship with her boyfriend. Her reticence was pathologized as "nonassertiveness" and confronted in the guise of "caring."

When Belinda realized that it was her work environment and not herself that was defective, her mood improved. She used her therapy to make her personal boundaries even stronger and to send the negative projections back where they belonged. She began to see her bosses as enfants terribles and to speak to them firmly but soothingly, as one would to a child. And she used her newfound energy to find another job.

2. Shame-Dumping and Scapegoating

In addition to the lack of boundaries in Belinda's work environment, there was also a high level of shame-dumping and scapegoating. This, in fact, was what had triggered Belinda's depressive symptoms, her usual confidence having been eroded by the not-so-subtle implication that she was flawed and, as a result, would probably be unable to perform her job adequately. Apart from being completely erroneous, where did that bizarre notion come from?

One can only speculate on the workings of her bosses' minds, but the clear evidence of their toxic narcissism suggests that they were projecting their intolerable envy and shame onto her, off-loading it to protect their own fragile egos. So what had triggered these feelings? Perhaps there was a glitch in one of her accounts, something that they felt made them or the company look bad. If she was stretched too thin or did not get adequate support and a deadline was missed, it would be necessary to find an explanation that did not make them look bad. Blaming Belinda outright might backfire, but expressing concern about her skills was a more subtle deflation that also allowed them to feel like "good parents." Even more likely, there was something in Belinda's quiet self-assurance—in the face of their frequent tantrums and lack of control—that made them feel inferior and had to be discredited. By making her composure a flaw, their own emotional outbursts became assertiveness, and their superiority was restored at her expense. Such distortions inevitably bear the hallmark of a narcissistic process and are crazy-making for the one on the receiving end.

A similar process is that of scapegoating. A particular employee becomes the receptacle of off-loaded shame and serves as a shame-regulator for the entire group. Often this is a person who is accustomed to this role, having received early training in the family. One can't help but wonder why, if this person is so inept, he or she is not simply dismissed. The answer is that such individuals perform an important function in a shame-laden environment. This is someone to whom everyone can feel superior.

3. The Grand Vision

Many employers use inspirational rhetoric and lofty goals to inspire and motivate employees, but in a toxic environment, the source of this "grand vision" is often the narcissistic leader's personal ambition to make fantasies of perfection come true by whipping subordinates into a frenzy of productivity. In such workplaces, people's private lives are cannibalized in the service of The Dream, and it is not unusual to see people putting in surreally long hours, sacrificing weekends and vacations, and coming to work sick. And they do it not just because they are afraid of losing their jobs, but also because their own emptied lives are inflated by their role in realizing the vision. The narcissistic fantasy captures the depleted in its net.

This is not just the need to get the job done. Often the very nature of the job has been redefined in perfectionistic terms by the narcissistic leader, and this becomes the new standard of adequacy. It is no longer a matter of feeling good if you are able to live up to these expectations, it's about feeling bad if you don't. Grandiosity sets the standard, and shame befalls those who don't measure up.

4. The Idealization of the Useful

Have you ever wondered how some people get to be "golden"? They may seem unremarkable, but for some reason, they garner more than their share of the goodies—commendations, promotions, special consideration regarding scheduling, office space or furniture, or other symbols of organizational status.

In a narcissistic environment, you need look no further than the powers-that-be to see how such dross is turned into precious metal. The answer is invariably that the fair-haired one somehow functions to make the boss look or feel more pumped up. The modestly skilled secretary who becomes a personal assistant or confidant to the boss is often a love interest, in fact or in fantasy, or has a special talent for soothing ruffled feathers or reflecting glory. The unremarkable line worker who is promoted to middle management may have been chosen precisely because she is mediocre and therefore can approach the throne without threatening the monarch. Often there is much hoopla upon a promotion about so-and-so's accomplishments, invoking considerable envy and contempt among overlooked coworkers who clearly see that the emperor's favorite has no clothes.

Never underestimate, however, the power of such a crown prince or princess. They may never ascend to the throne, but only the monarch can cause them to fall from grace. Their position is utterly dependent on their usefulness to their liege, and they may be demoted at will or protected indefinitely. Some of these people become appendages to the Narcissist, following him or her from job to job throughout a career. Regardless of what you think of their actual merits, it is wise to treat them with respect.

5. Shameless Exploitation

The narcissistic leader is typically single-minded in the pursuit of power and recognition for specialness and feels entitled to these rewards. Deception, distortion, and seduction are among the tools of the trade, to be used without compunction whenever needed. The only shame is failure, and nothing, least of all empathy for subordinates, stands in the Narcissist's way. Often the degree of ruthlessness and emotional detachment is disguised behind a mask of propriety and unctuous solicitude, but in some organizational subcultures, boldness is itself a badge of honor. In such environments, anything goes, and a subordinate can expect to be used mercilessly, criticized liberally for whatever disappoints or deflates the leader, and summarily dismissed when no longer needed. The practice of stretching employees until they break and then getting rid of them has become so common that it even has a name: "rubber band management."

All of this creates an environment saturated with fear and mistrust. In the worst situations, paranoia becomes good judgment. The real danger is the insidious way that remaining in such a brutal situation erodes the self-worth of the exploited. When you are whipped into a constant frenzy and expendable and disposable to boot, you may find that time for a personal life isn't all that's in short supply. So are your confidence, your joy, and your emotional energy.

6. Mood Swings from Elation to Rage

Some narcissistic leaders are models of icy reserve while others have the emotional self-control of a two-year-old. This tendency toward volatility is often associated with young leaders in glamorous or high-tech industries—the so-called "bratty bunch"—but the essential narcissistic defect is not something people generally outgrow. In fact, narcissism may become more entrenched with age and expanding power. To the extent that power becomes more secure, the moody Narcissist may have more insulation from the shame that is the principal regulator of bad behavior. The more powerful you are, the more you can get away with.

Some badly behaved leaders evoke sympathy from others who erroneously attribute their mood swings to stress. While the demands of leadership can, at times, push people over the edge, the screaming, pouting, mind games, and manic excitement that characterize the moody narcissistic leader have more to do with their infantile personalities than with acute stress. Such people never developed the ability to calm themselves, and their unrealistic expectations and need to control what is often uncontrollable can keep them in a constant state of agitation.

If you and others feel you must walk on eggshells to avoid setting off a landmine, suspect underlying narcissism and tailor your responses accordingly.

7. Envy

The amount of envy, open or concealed, in a given organization is often a good measure of the level of narcissism in its power structure. Envy has its roots in the toddler's crushed omnipotence, the sudden painful awareness of lacking what Mother or Father has. The envious one subconsciously wishes to spoil or destroy that which evokes feelings of inferiority. It is a common feeling in lopsided power relationships and the emotional trigger behind the gossip, backbiting, and boot-licking that are prevalent in many work environments.

It is also a common feeling among Narcissists, who are keenly sensitive to potential shifts in the balance of power. Envy is often expressed in put-downs or competitive oneupmanship but may also be the driving force behind excessive praise. By showing contempt, the envious demean that which makes them feel diminished. By competing, they strive to capture what is desired for their own while elevating themselves at another's expense. Insincere praise is a way of denying contemptuous feelings to oneself and others, as well as avoiding the shame that feeling envious evokes. Any or all of these actions reveal envy, and possibly a Narcissist.

Excessive praise also has another meaning. Since awareness of envy evokes shame, envy is projected onto others, who then become feared. "I don't envy him; he envies me, and I'd better butter him up or he'll be out to get me." Praise is offered as a way of bribing a potential rival not to retaliate against one's own perceived superiority. Psychologically, this is a complicated pas de deux, but to the observer, it just looks like fawning. When you see this kind of obsequious behavior from a Narcissist in power, you are watching envy in action.

The narcissistic leader's idealization of favorites and tendency to criticize, blame, and scapegoat creates an atmosphere of envy among subordinates as well. High expectations and the promise of rewards, however illusory they might be, also stimulate competition within the ranks and make everyone anxious and fearful of "looking bad."

8. Admiration-Seeking

On the other end of the same continuum from envy is the narcissistic leader's need to feel admired, which is nothing more than the craving for narcissistic supplies. Behavior that says "Pump me up!" is a sign of momentary insecurity that must be handled deftly lest the leader become aware of having exposed a weakness. Sensitive underlings who wish to stay in the master's good graces learn to intuit when a "Bravo!" is needed. Generally, the more secure the Narcissist is in his power, the less he trolls for approval among his subordinates, although pouting after a deflation is a signal to the wise. The insecure leader, on the other hand, can be really draining, and it can feel like a full-time job just propping him up without shaming him. In any event, the well-timed compliment or show of appreciation is always a hit with the narcissistic boss.

Caught in the Web: How Narcissists Seduce Us

Sometimes life just seems a little humdrum, a little flat. When you haven't felt excitement or motivation for a while, there's nothing like a little narcissism to perk you up.

Narcissists, who are convinced of their own specialness, often exude a special charm that makes others feel pumped up, too—at least initially. When they shine their light on you, even for only a brief moment, you may walk away feeling happier, more inspired, or just elevated in some indescribable way. It is as if you have been sprinkled with pixie dust, and life just feels a little brighter.

This only happens, however, if they want you for something. If they have no use for you, you might as well be invisible. That can be painful, even if you don't really care about the person, because you see the light shining on others and feel left out of the glow. Your exclusion may have a deflating effect on you.

The aura that surrounds the Narcissist often creates envy and competition. You may be aware, on some level, of wanting to be part of what's going on, regardless of whether you actually like the person or not. The process of being deflated and the opportunity to be inflated (if you can capture the Narcissist's attention in some positive way) may have all entered your life unbidden. It is within the Narcissist's power to create this atmosphere simply by manipulating others' experiences of inflation and deflation. Even if you choose not to participate or react, you cannot help but feel it. Next time you are in the presence of someone whom you suspect is narcissistic, test yourself. Chances are that even if you see through the mask to the insecure person within, you will feel pumped up if that person smiles on you and contemptuous (envious, deflated) if he or she does not.

What the Narcissist is doing, sometimes even without awareness, is playing with your narcissistic vulnerability. The more shame-sensitive you are, the more you will feel the ebb and flow of inflation-deflation. If you grew up in a family with a narcissistic parent or parents, you have buttons just waiting to be pushed. You have the potential to become a veritable keyboard for the Narcissist to play at will, pumping you up and putting you down as it suits his or her needs. Narcissistic processes always have the same outcome: You get your hopes built up, you get your hopes dashed. It will never be about you.

Those who will have the most difficulty with Narcissists in power are those narcissistically vulnerable souls who are defending their egos at every turn. These are the people who often have difficulty with authority in general and do poorly in hierarchical structures where they are not in command. If the authority is also a Narcissist, the misery will be intolerable. Better to find a job in a more benign environment or one with a high degree of autonomy and control. The essence of being able to manage the Narcissist is to transcend your own ego. Only the most self-assured (or previously programmed) are likely to succeed at this daunting task.

A Tale of Two Kitties

Once upon a time, there were two clever and ambitious young cats who went to work for a proud and wily lion. "Welcome to my company," said the lion expansively. "You are now among the chosen few. We hire only the very best, because the work here is very important and we have a reputation to maintain. Work hard, and you will share in my glory. But if you disappoint me, I will send you away with your tails dragging!"

The two young cats were very excited about their good fortune and sure that they could please the lion and advance their careers. They pranced about with their heads held high and felt just a little bit superior to the other felines. They didn't tell anyone, however, that their wages were stingy and their hours very long. What mattered was that they were valued employees of the lion's important company. "I see a big future for myself here," said the sleek black one. "This is my dream job," echoed the pretty little tabby.

Each worked very hard, trying her best to keep the lion happy. Sometimes he lavished praise on them, and sometimes he ignored them or flew into a rage at the slightest deviation from his wishes. As they got to know more of what went on behind the scenes, they discovered that the company's prestigious image was largely an illusion created by the lion and maintained by those who served him. Knowing this, each of the little cats saw an opportunity.

"I will have some of this power for myself," said the sleek black one. "If I show the lion how talented I am, he will share his power with me." And she began to plot. "But the lion does not want to share his power," said the pretty little tabby. "I will work hard to make him look good, and he will depend on me."

In time, they both achieved their goals. The sleek black cat so impressed the lion with her innovative ideas that he wanted to harness her talent for his own purposes. Just as she had predicted, he promoted her and promoted her again, grooming her to be the cat who sat at his big right paw. Everyone treated her with respect, and she became very bold and sure of herself.

In the meantime, the pretty little tabby was busy making her own, different way. She worked tirelessly, sometimes into the night, to polish the lion's image and make sure that it was always burnished to a luster for all the world to admire. Although she often made personal sacrifices, she never asked for a thing for herself in return. In fact, whenever the spotlight chanced to shine on her corner of the company, she always found a way to redirect its beam onto the lion. He was endlessly pleased with his pretty little kitty and spared her much of the criticism he often found for his other employees.

He began to feel uneasy about the sleek black cat, however. Her creativity, which once had reflected so well on him, now seemed threatening. He noticed the way others had begun to treat her with deference, and he became convinced that he must neutralize her power somehow. But when he tried to control her, he suddenly realized how important she had become to him. His need astonished him and made him feel vulnerable, foolish, and inept. Shame and helplessness flooded over him and turned into an ugly rage. When he could stand it no longer, he fired her, throwing the company into immediate chaos. "It is all her fault," he roared, and for a time thereafter, the mere mention of her name would curl his mighty lip in contempt.

The destabilization of the company and the ensuing threat to the lion's image caused the pretty little tabby to have to go to work overtime to ensure damage control, but once again, she rose to the challenge without so much as a moment of self-pity or complaint. Still, her efforts had begun to wear on her, and she was tired. When word of her quiet devotion spread throughout the community, she was offered a position in another company and, to everyone's surprise, she took it. The lion was devastated. "Stay with me," he pleaded, "and I will give you three bags of gold." "You are so gracious," said the pretty little tabby, "but it is time for me to move on." And so she did, to a peaceful job with normal hours.

When we enter the realm of the Narcissist, the feeling of excitement can be almost palpable. "Something special happens here," we tell ourselves, "and I want to be part of it." That heady feeling is a signal that our own narcissism has been awakened, and we have been invited to fuse with the illusory world of the Narcissist in power. Enter at your own risk, for like Alice walking through the looking glass, you will find the world on the other side is full of deceptions, distortions, and dangers.

It is ironic that the very thing that has drawn us into this fantasy place, our own need for inflation, is the first thing that must be relinquished. If you are unable to do that, the fate that awaits you is the one that befell the sleek black cat. Allow your ego to feed on the fantasy that you, too, will acquire power, and whatever you create will be destroyed. You will find out in the end that there is only room for one ego, only one can hold the reins of power. And unless there is some reversal of fortune, it won't be you.

The ones who are able to survive and even, sometimes, to prevail in the power world of the Narcissist are those, like the pretty little tabby, who can transcend their own egos and perfect the art of serving the master. Often these are closet Narcissists who are adept at inflating others and redirecting the limelight away from themselves, content to bask in another's glow. Because they can seamlessly manipulate the Narcissist's need for admiration, they often acquire a subtle power of their own, which they wield through seduction, suggestion, and influence. They pose no threat, provoke no shame, and cause neither envy nor contempt. They are utterly soothing.

Guidelines for Survival with a Narcissist in Power

Strategy One: Know Yourself

Working in a narcissistic environment will put your own vulnerabilities to the test. If you come from a narcissistic family, are acutely sensitive to shaming, need other people to admire you in order to feel good about yourself, or rely primarily on your job to give you a sense of self-worth, you are in for a rough ride. How much can you handle? Know yourself!

In order to play in the Narcissist's game, you must be in control of your own narcissistic triggers. Be sure that you can keep inflation in check and curb your tendencies to idealize and lose touch with reality. Plan how you will keep from being seduced by the Narcissist's illusions, as they are invariably self-serving, often manipulative, and usually not in your best interests. Most of all, develop a strategy for managing your anger when you are inevitably used and abused by the Narcissist. Recognize when you are building up a head of steam and don't allow yourself to react until you've had a chance to process your feelings and your options with a neutral person, preferably someone outside the workplace. You will need a great deal of self-awareness and self-control to stay in this game.

Strategy Two: Embrace Reality

Understand clearly what you are dealing with. The workplace is not a family environment. Your boss is not a protective father or a nurturing mother, regardless of how the situation has been presented to you. When the power structure is narcissistic, however, your rivalries with coworkers may have a distinctly sibling feel. Try to hold yourself above the fray.

Know the Narcissist's weakness, the fragile Self beneath the mask of superiority and power. Become sensitive to what triggers his or her shame and envy. Learn to read the meaning behind the grandiosity, arrogance, need for admiration, entitlement, contempt, and rage. Then treat the Narcissist as you would a small, vulnerable child—but with twice the respect.

Be careful not to do anything that offends or challenges the Narcissist's images or illusions. Remember that he or she is not interested in truth, reality, or you. If you inadvertently deflate, be prepared to do damage control. Know what works and what doesn't.

If you wish to avoid evoking envy, you must never compete for attention with the Narcissist. Unfortunately, this may mean minimizing your talents and accomplishments and allowing the Narcissist to take credit for what you do. If you wish to prevail, learn to suck it up and keep a low profile. Cultivate the art of seamlessly blending in—be vague, bland, and inconspicuous when not in the service of the Narcissist.

Conversely, you may wish to learn to inflate and soothe the Narcissist. Do this by using flattery and becoming a source of pleasure whenever the opportunity arises. This is likely to make the Narcissist dependent on you, so you must be careful not to let your intentions show. If the Narcissist becomes aware of being dependent, humiliation can follow quickly and you will feel the sting of narcissistic rage. So if you want to be indispensable, be sure to be nonthreatening as well.

Learn to recognize the signs of envy: criticism and excessive praise. Should you inadvertently evoke envy despite your best efforts, you can dampen your own brilliance by revealing a flaw or weakness, or you can credit luck for your "good fortune." Remember that your accomplishments, when not in the service of the Narcissist, threaten and diminish him or her. They become narcissistic injuries, for which you will pay. Never forget that you are connected to the Narcissist in ways that you cannot see—you are an extension of that person's ego. You must never outshine the Narcissist.

Recognize and avoid the power traps, such as vagueness or inspirational rhetoric, that the Narcissist sets for you. Learn to see through the illusions to reality. Be on guard for hidden motives, and be cautious with your trust.

Strategy Three: Set Boundaries

To labor in the service of a Narcissist is to face many challenges to your personal boundaries. Anticipate how you will respond to these assaults so you won't be caught off-guard, and once you have set a limit, be prepared to defend it, firmly and calmly, with as few words and as little emotion as possible.

Recognize off-loaded shame for what it is, the Narcissist's mechanism for restoring his or her own internal equilibrium. Try not to personalize attacks; develop a psychological shield by converting your feelings to thought processes. Know why you feel what you feel and remember, mentally, to send the shame back where it came from. When you develop the ability to depersonalize and detach, you form an internal protective boundary.

While learning to read the Narcissist's behavior, practice being unreadable yourself. Maintain an inner aloofness by withholding your private Self. The piece of you that remains unknowable and unobtainable is your personal power base. Guard it carefully, but don't be too mysterious, as those who keep others guessing also risk making them feel inferior. Create an image of your own to manage your circumstances and keep yourself intact behind the mask. Think of yourself as an actor in a play.

Beware of the excesses of deliberate self-abdication. Allowing the Narcissist to feed on you at your own expense (as opposed to nibbling on an image that you have concocted) is very risky to your self-esteem. You must have truly permeable boundaries or an unhealthy need to experience humiliation to engage in what can quickly become a sadomasochistic relationship. Know the limits of your own tolerance, and protect yourself.

Try to build and maintain a firm boundary between work and your personal life. Leave the deceptions, distortions, and deflations behind you when you go home.

Strategy Four: Cultivate Reciprocal Relationships

To neutralize the power the Narcissist has over your career, develop your own power base, the wider the better. Align yourself with other sources of power within the Narcissist's sphere of influence, if possible, and privately document abuses and excesses. You never know when the documentation will come in handy to get you out of a predicament. Maintain relationships outside the organization. One day, you may decide to bail out.

Consider the costs of remaining in the Narcissist's power arena. It takes a great deal of energy for most healthy people to maintain the selfless persona necessary to manage proximity to a powerful Narcissist. What are you getting for what you're giving up? How has this changed you? What impact has this had on your intimate relationships, your ability to function as a parent, spouse, lover, or friend? Is it worth it?

You need to be especially attentive to creating healthy relationships in your private life. You will need the support of people you can trust to help you stay grounded in reality, to process the distortions, and to shake off the shame that may be dumped on you at work.

● ● ●

To survive in an environment dominated by a Narcissist, you will need to be on your toes at all times. You must be aware of your "hooks" and curb your own narcissistic tendencies to idealize and chase rainbows. You must never forget who you're dealing with or the limits of your own power and authority. You must create barriers to protect yourself from the Narcissist's web. And you must cultivate healthy relationships to provide emotional insulation and counteract the impact of toxic narcissism.

Many of these coping strategies, adapted from time-tested truths about the nature of power relationships, are manipulative and deceptive. They require that you, like the Narcissist, create and control your own image, and that you know the difference between your image and your real Self. When dealing with a Narcissist who has power over you, it is naive to expect to be yourself and not be eaten alive. It is healthy to want to be in an environment that is free of exploitation, distortion, and shame. Unfortunately, those power structures that reward unhealthy narcissism will never be such safe places. If you can't stand the heat, it is up to you to get out of the kitchen.

18

Narcissism and Aging: The Mirror Cracks

AGING IS THE ULTIMATE NARCISSISTIC INJURY. Many of the mirrors that validated worthiness can no longer be counted on to reflect back the same reassuring images. The thinning hair, the sagging flesh, the mind that dumps thoughts and takes too long to retrieve them, the aches and pains that may signal unspeakable terrors yet to come, are evidence that the supply lines for maintaining inflation are drying up. Nothing works like it used to, and everything is changing, out of control. Roles shift, and the sphere of influence shrinks. People move on, die. Power goes with them and leaves loneliness in its wake.

The Narcissist typically meets these challenges with denial. If a face-lift or a tummy tuck or a hair transplant is within the budget, it must be had. Pushing the physical limits to prove that one still has "the right stuff" has become a commonplace pursuit in our narcissistic world. Fast cars and young lovers can also keep the illusion alive for a time. But when denial finally begins to break down, when the cracks in the mirror can no longer be ignored, what we are likely to see is an increase in certain nasty behavior that may have been present all along but now becomes more prominent. Primitive envy and defensive devaluation of others are both desperate attempts to maintain a sense of superiority and restore lost emotional equilibrium.

Dinner with Deirdre

Deirdre was holding court again at the dining room table. The seventy-year-old matriarch convened these gatherings on a regular basis to keep an eye on her three "darling" sons and their "dreadful" wives and to make sure that they all took home with them a piece of her mind.

Deirdre had been widowed for more than three decades, and her departed husband had left her financially secure. The twelve years of their marriage had apparently been enough for her, as she had never found a suitable suitor to take his place. The companionship of her "three little men" had sustained her, at least until the boys had started getting married. Her only regret now was that they had not been more discriminating in their choice of mates.

Peter's wife, Mandy, was perhaps the worst. They had never had children, and she fancied herself quite the career woman. Not that she needed to work; Peter had done quite well for himself and could give Mandy anything she wanted—and usually did. Mandy was full of opinions and never shut up. Deirdre hated the way Mandy looked her straight in the eye and, after all these years, still didn't know her place. Poor Peter—Deirdre couldn't imagine why he put up with such a know-it-all.

Tom's wife, Linda, was just the opposite, but nearly as insufferable. A mousy little thing who had gained more weight with each of her four pregnancies and never even tried to reclaim her figure, she had no taste in clothing or anything else and no control over her brood of children, two things that Deirdre absolutely could not abide. Most of all, however, Deirdre hated the way that Tom looked at his wife when he thought no one else was watching. It was embarrassing, really, her beautiful son with such a sow.

Then there was the newest addition to the family, Benjamin's third wife, Elise. Deirdre had not been sorry to see the other two go, but if she had known what was in store, she might have intervened to prevent the last divorce. At least number two had been close to Ben's age. This one was considerably younger, and she wore both her hair and her skirts too short, had wretched table manners, and talked like an idiot. There was no other word to describe Elise except common. With luck, Benjamin would tire of her, too.

Deirdre looked around the table and sighed, barely able to control the disgust she was feeling. The women avoided eye contact with her and her sons braced themselves, knowing from experience that when she stiffened her back and the corners of her mouth turned down, an attack was imminent. Who would be the target? Would she bait Mandy with a snide question about her job, or humiliate Linda by comparing her children's accomplishments to those of their father, or remind Elise to start with the outside fork? Shame was nearly always the first course when the family sat down to dinner with Deirdre.

Deirdre's contempt for her daughters-in-law reflects a malignant envy of the place they now hold in her sons' lives, a place that she once could claim as exclusively her own. Notice, too, how her sons are spared from her verbal assaults while the women can do nothing right in her eyes. This is another characteristic of the emotionally imma- ture, the tendency to "split" others into categories of "all good" and "all bad." Under certain circumstances, the "good" can become the "bad," or vice versa, but no one is ever seen accurately as having both good and bad qualities at the same time. Narcissists cannot tolerate si- multaneously loving and hateful feelings toward the same person, which is why their relationships often resemble a roller-coaster ride of inflation and deflation. As the Narcissist ages, these idealizations and devaluations of needed others can become more dramatic.

A man I know well was doted on by his elderly maiden aunt, a brittle narcissistic type with a reputation for haughtiness and gratuitous slurs. That she never had children of her own and he lost his mother at a relatively young age had made their bond a special one, but it didn't quite explain why this imperious woman turned to jelly, all batting eyelashes and girlish giggles, whenever her nephew was around. He, of course, could see the discrepancy between how she valued him and her usual contempt for others, but he just shook his head in wonder. He knew she could be treacherous, but he thought he was immune.

Then one day, in the course of trying to help her through a difficult period in her life, he opposed her irrational wishes. In a flash, he discovered what it was like to be on the receiving end of her wrath. She called him deceitful and malevolent, and she threatened to summon her attorney to protect herself against his perceived aggression. The beloved nephew had not just fallen off a pedestal, he had ceased to exist in her mind. Then, just as quickly as she had turned on him, it was over and he was back in her good graces. They never spoke of this stain on their relationship, but if they had, she might very well have denied that any unpleasantness had ever occurred.

The paranoia sometimes seen in elderly Narcissists represents a defense against depression of psychotic proportions. Unable to maintain a self-concept of superiority, the aging Narcissist collapses inside and succumbs to fears of being invaded by vengeful, annihilating forces that will prey on him in his weakened, dependent state. He must be watchful and wary. Narratives about spiteful others who are intent on wreaking havoc are a last-ditch effort to salvage a sense of control over the terror of helplessness and dependency. Unfortunately for the poor Narcissist, however, these rantings only serve to further alienate those on whom he must depend, leading to even more dehumanization and emptiness. When everything that has sustained grandiosity and omnipotence collapses, both the fragile Self and the world lose meaning, and despair may give way to a psychotic depression that provides the only remaining pathway to comforting illusion. Painful reality is replaced by madness.

Most elderly Narcissists don't implode quite so completely but instead may hover above total insanity in a state of fearful self-preoccupation. The aches and pains of an aging body can become magnified into near hysteria, and the resulting panic may be immobilizing. Here's what it looked like to one daughter:

Maureen: Life on the Screen

Maureen was exasperated with her father's helpless behavior. Ever since his wife's death two years before, the seventy-five-year-old patriarch seemed unable to do anything for himself. Although he stubbornly refused to listen to advice about his investment portfolio, he was utterly at a loss to balance his own checkbook. He couldn't lift a finger around the house, but he complained that the housekeepers Maureen hired were lazy or stealing from him, and he'd fire each one and demand another. It seemed to her that nearly every day he would become frustrated at some simple task and ring her up, expecting her to drop whatever she was doing and come immediately to his aid. If she tried to offer suggestions or encouragement over the phone, he became petulant. The worst calls were the ones in the middle of the night, when he interrupted her sleep with fears that he couldn't breathe or was having a heart attack. Finding him fit as a fiddle, his doctor had suggested that he take medication for anxiety, but he refused.

Although she alone among his four children had helped to make the funeral arrangements for their mother, to dispose of Mother's personal effects, and to sell the couple's vacation home, nothing Maureen did for her father ever seemed to be enough. He never thanked her or showed interest in or concern about her life, but he complained bitterly if she disappointed him in any way.

Maureen had tried to set aside her hurt feelings about the way her father had treated her mother while she was dying, but the images continued to haunt her—of her father's indifference to her mother's pain, of his anger at her increasing dependency, of his refusal to assist in her care. She had been particularly stung by his criticism of her mother and his offhand comments on the day of the funeral about wanting to meet someone new.

She had always known that he could be remote and difficult, but she had never imagined him to be so uncaring.

Lately, his cruelty had become more pointedly directed toward her. He had begun to accuse Maureen of meddling and blamed her when things were missing from his house. At a party she hosted for the family, he openly criticized her lifestyle and made negative remarks about her in front of her children and behind her back to her sisters. He also went to unprecedented lengths to ingratiate himself with his other daughters, flashing the charm that he was capable of on occasion. Maureen felt that she had somehow become the enemy, and completely alone in the family. She knew, however, that when her sisters returned to their homes in other states, her father would continue to look to her to meet his every need. She was left with no way out of the aggravation, and no one to understand or share her burden.

Maureen's father exhibits the classic entitlement, exploitation, and lack of empathy that are among the Seven Deadly Sins of Narcissism. His excessive demands and the absence of interest in her as a separate person reveal his profound lack of boundaries. Although he seems to want to control everything, he also acts out his helplessness, projecting it onto Maureen's "screen." It's strange how that works—the more helpless he becomes, the more he is able to control Maureen and make *her* feel helpless. If he can make her own what he fears most, he doesn't have to feel it so much himself. He can use her to bypass the shame of his own deflated Self. Maureen has inherited her mother's role as regulator of her father's internal state, and like Mother, she must be held in contempt for having become the container of his disowned Self.

It is tempting to want to make excuses for an elderly man who has lost his wife. Surely, he is depressed, fearful, and bewildered at the necessary adjustments to living alone. Perhaps he can't balance his own checkbook because he is losing his mental faculties or suffering from an undiagnosed medical condition. Of course, he must depend on his family to look after him. Isn't any elderly person entitled to that?

Indeed, the aging Narcissist has the same needs for compassion, assistance, and respectful care that anyone deserves toward the end of life. That fact, however, does not negate what a primary caretaker— usually a daughter or son who has suffered a parent's narcissism from early childhood—must cope with as narcissistic traits escalate to warp speed and threaten to annihilate whatever Self the adult child has been able to mobilize in the contrail of such a parent. Alongside the frailty and dependency that come with aging, the elderly Narcissist has some special qualities that belong to Narcissists alone. The boundary between their real and defensive needs often becomes quite difficult to discern. Perhaps that is because their defensive needs have never been so desperately real.

Guidelines for Survival for Adult Children of Aging Narcissists

Strategy One: Know Yourself

When does "aging" begin? Is it when one first notices a gray hair or a wrinkle, when one can't eat what one usually does without gaining weight, when one can't see as well or tires and aches more easily, or when one can no longer compete with younger people for the things that maintain a sense of well-being? For your narcissistic parent, that process may have begun when you were still a child, and the resultant denial, devaluation of others, envy, self-preoccupation, and paranoia may have been a part of your experience of that parent for as long as you can remember. What can you identify now as your parent's response to aging, and how did that affect you?

It is important to understand this, because these are the same buttons that are going to be pushed as both you and your parent continue to age. Were you and your accomplishments ignored or devalued because your parent couldn't compete with you? Were you expected to function as an auxiliary in some process that pumped him or her up?

Did you develop fears about your own health or appearance because of a parent's panic about growing older?

You have survived childhood with a narcissistic parent and now have more options than you once did for taking control of your own life. You are no longer dependent in the same way you were, although you may still be carrying around inside of you pieces of your parent that you have trouble distinguishing from yourself. You can do something about this—you can become your own separate person.

Take stock of your assets and what belongs to you that you can use to continue your growth toward separation and health. Consider what coping strategies you have used and which ones have been good for you and which ones destructive. What do you need to mobilize in your life to remain on a healthy path?

If you decide to maintain contact with your narcissistic parent, you will need to begin to examine the process of that relationship, paying special attention to how you get "hooked" into re-enacting your role in the narcissistic drama. What are your buttons? How are they triggered? Once again, insight and self-control are your first lines of defense.

If you find yourself in a caretaking role with an elderly Narcissist, examine in particular your feelings about nurturance, dependency, and power. The old roles have been reversed, and that may be as difficult for you as it is for your parent. The caretaking role demands that you nurture this person who may never have nurtured you—how do you really feel about dependency, your own or someone else's? What power does your parent still have over you, and how will that affect your ability to be "in charge" when the time comes? How will you cope with the feelings evoked by your parent's escalating defenses—the denial, envy and contempt, manipulativeness, hostility, demands, panic, paranoia, and irrationality? Coping with an elderly narcissistic parent can be an aggravating and exhausting ordeal. The better you understand yourself and the process that goes on between you—a process that involves other members of the family and the circle of your parent's friends and associates—the more manageable this will become.

Strategy Two: Embrace Reality

Understanding why your parent acts the way he or she does is an essential first step toward being able to manage the challenges of an aging Narcissist, but what may be more difficult for you is actually accepting these truths. This is because to accept the truth of your parent's primitive internal world means giving up hope of ever being recognized and valued as a separate person.

Not all Narcissists are the same, nor will they behave the same in old age. And aging raises narcissistic issues for us all. Those who have some tolerance for sadness and anxiety, who have been fundamentally honest and fair in their dealings with others throughout their lives, who have reasonable impulse control, who do not abuse substances, and who can sustain relationships while growing more dependent and perhaps continue to find narcissistic supplies in their shrinking world may be able, with empathic support, to adapt to the realities of old age. If you are able to recognize their need for mirroring and idealization and provide them with carefully attuned feedback and support, they may be able to sustain an inflated image of both themselves and you that will hold the demons at bay.

What this means in practical day-to-day parlance is that you make yourself available to meet certain of their emotional, as well as functional, needs. Without being condescending, you acknowledge their accomplishments and victories, however small. You are nonconfrontational in your dealings with them and avoid shaming them at all costs. That may mean *not* talking about your own accomplishments or good fortune or those of others among your mutual acquaintances, because to do so triggers envy. To the extent that it is reasonably possible, you allow them to maintain as much control as possible over their own lives. You try to understand them accurately, which may mean *not* filtering their words and behavior through the prism of your lifelong experience with them or others like them. You avoid assigning blame and manage feelings of hurt, anger, or disappointment apart from them. You do not try to change them at this late stage. You approach them with compassion even when they are being difficult, or you accept that someone else may be better able to deal with these things than you are, even if this disappoints your expectations of yourself. You let go of the hope that this will ever be a reciprocal relationship, and in doing so, you may find the gift of peace, with yourself and with your narcissistic parent.

There are among Narcissists some who cannot be managed by a son or a daughter with whom they share a lifetime of toxic emotional entanglements. Personality theorist Otto Kernberg called "malignant" those Narcissists whose grandiosity is built around aggression and destruction of those who offer love. These are sadistic, antisocial types with a deeply paranoid orientation toward life who so idealize their own aggressive power that they have killed off the sane and loving parts of themselves that might have enabled them to develop attachments and tolerate dependence. They wish only to destroy, symbolically castrate, and dehumanize others, and their paranoia may become so intense in old age that they are virtually unapproachable. If your parent falls into this category, it is better to deal from a distance. Your illusions of possible softening and reunion in old age could be dangerous to your emotional health and well-being.

Another way to embrace reality is to create a mantra for yourself with the following message: "There is nothing I can do to change my narcissistic parent. I can never be perfect or pleasing enough to win his or her unconditional or consistent love. His or her inability to love and respect me has nothing to do with my value as a human being. The more I cling to my idealized fantasies of becoming perfect and having an ideal parent, the more I hurt myself. I will seek to discover my own uniqueness and to connect with people who are capable of recognizing me and accepting me for who I am. I am worthy of the love my parent was unable to give me."

When you interact with your parent, see him or her as he or she really is. Accept this person's limitations and appreciate his or her gifts. Let your realistic assessment of your parent and your own internal reality dictate your involvement.

Strategy Three: Set Boundaries

If you choose to interact with a narcissistic parent, it will be helpful to impose some limits, both on how you handle yourself and on what you will tolerate from your parent. To begin, identify behavior or situations that make you feel angry or out of control. Does your parent attack you directly, or are the barbs generally aimed at others, such as your spouse, siblings, or children? Do you feel used, unappreciated, or the object of unreasonable expectations? Does your parent's anxiety, negativity, or irritability drive you nuts? Have you fallen into the trap of supplying reassurances that never seem to matter?

You will need to find a way to distance yourself from the emotional "hooks" that cause you to feel angry, defensive, and depleted or ineffectual. Try reframing the things your parent says as having a positive rather than a negative intent. If, for example, you convert criticism to "help," you now perceive your mother as showing "concern" about your difficulty holding a job, and the element of victimization is eliminated. Even if you don't believe that she is trying to be helpful, to respond to her this way meets her need to feel important without sacrificing your dignity. If you are used to defending yourself or others in a hurt or angry way, this will feel very different. The difference is that you are in control, putting a stop not to her behavior but to your experience of it.

You can try to ask your parent to refrain from certain behavior while in your presence, and this may or may not work. What is valuable about asserting yourself in this way, however, is not so much your effectiveness in getting your parent to change as the experience of standing up for yourself even if your wishes are ignored. If you have always been intimidated by your narcissistic parent, it can be good for you to test how the balance of power may have shifted. You might even choose to set some limits. Tell Mom or Dad, calmly, what you are prepared to do if you are not respected. Be sure, however, that the consequence is something you will be willing to enforce, because once you have set a boundary, you must not back off. It is better to test the waters around smaller issues than to make a grand stand in a moment of anger that you will later regret. If this sounds a lot like dealing with children, it's because it is. As New York City psychologist and author Elan Golomb advises, you will need to master the art of "noncombative firmness" and practice "bland indifference" to provocation in order to insulate yourself emotionally and maintain your equilibrium. Expect this to take some practice.

Do not allow your narcissistic parent to manipulate you through guilt and shame. It is up to you to examine your own conscience and decide what responsibilities you choose to accept. There are many ways to honor your parent short of sacrificing your own life and well-being and that of your loved ones. You do not need to succumb to unreasonable demands in order to be a good son or daughter. It is all right to say "No" or to mobilize others who may be better able to meet your parent's needs with less drama. You have as much of an obligation to yourself and to the others who depend on you as you do to your narcissistic parent, and you are entitled to set your own priorities without being manipulated by those who feel their claim on you should supersede all others.

Finally, try to come to decisions about what you will and won't tolerate from your parent *before* situations arise. Do whatever is necessary to protect yourself and know that you have a right to do this. Then whatever you decide to do, *do it as nondefensively as you can.*

Strategy Four: Cultivate Reciprocal Relationships

It goes without saying that if you are actively involved in caring for an elderly Narcissist, you will need the support of others to help you maintain your sense of balance and worth. Don't ignore reciprocity in these relationships by neglecting the needs of your support system, or you only pass along the narcissistic drain. Take time to show appreciation, and take breaks from your activities with the Narcissist to be genuinely present and participate in the lives of those who love you.

To recover from the wounds of parental narcissism and to ensure that an elderly narcissistic parent receives adequate care in his or her later years, it may be necessary to shake up the family. Everyone in a family system has a role assigned to them by someone else, usually the parents. If you have been the designated caretaker, or the scapegoat, or the "defective one," or even "the achiever," you will have to show your relatives that there is more to you than they previously thought. Treat others with respect, acknowledge their feelings and needs, and insist that they do the same toward you. Be firm and persistent. These things do not change overnight, and often there is much resistance. Know that regardless of whether your family can rise to the challenge of health, you can change yourself and how you relate to them. Insist on reciprocity, but if you cannot find it among your relatives, look elsewhere. You can create your own "second family" composed of friends whom you choose because together, you support one another's healthy separateness. These are the relationships that will sustain you over time and help prepare you for your own final act. No matter how torturous old age is or was for your narcissistic parent, you can avoid the same fate by loving and letting love in.

If you are able to make peace with your narcissistic parent, to give without feeling taken advantage of, to love even though you may receive little in return, to accept what never was and can never be, you will be free to search elsewhere for the reciprocity you deserve.

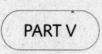

PART V

Only You Can Prevent Narcissism

19

The Narcissistic Society

NARCISSISM IN ITS MOST PERVASIVE FORM is a serious mental illness that affects a person's self-concept, attitudes, moods, behavior, relationships, and prospects for productivity and happiness. It afflicts not only those who carry the diagnosis but also those who live and work with such people, and especially those who love and are dependent on them. There is no pill to make it go away, and it tends to grow worse with age. At its most malignant, it is not even particularly treatable, because to benefit from the psychotherapy that could prove healing, the Narcissist first has to accept that there is something defective about the Self, and that is precisely what he or she cannot do.

Although full-blown Narcissistic Personality Disorder is still considered rather unusual, its traits and symptoms are common enough that many of us encounter unhealthy narcissism in some form nearly every day. In fact, it seems to have permeated our culture in ways that reinforce individual pathology while simultaneously making it look almost normal. What becomes normal in the culture is then passed along to our children through the institutions and influences that shape their minds and character. While it is true that the most potent transmitter of narcissism from one generation to the next is parenting, individual parents and families find themselves fighting an uphill battle to raise healthy children in a world that is saturated with narcissistic images and values. And many parents have simply given up trying.

Although sociologists began commenting on cultural narcissism over twenty-five years ago, the "Me Decade" didn't end in the 1980s, and the "Me Generation" spawned its own brood of self-absorbed entitlement monsters. If you look around you, you'll see that the Seven Deadly Sins are not just a matter of individual pathology but are social phenomena that have kept cultural narcissism alive and thriving into the new millennium.

Lack of Boundaries and the Denial of Limits

Intuitively, we recognize that we need secure parameters in order to function effectively, yet we routinely ignore boundaries or view them as obstacles to be overcome. Science has allowed us to defy gravity, transcend time and space, slow aging, cheat death, and even create life. We have been seduced into believing that there should be no limits, yet without them there is chaos and unreality. The current recipe for innovation involves "thinking outside the box," and a modern cowboy who defies the rules is still our idea of a hero. The need to be grounded in reality seems stuffy and old-fashioned by comparison. We prefer images of unlimited possibilities that feed our grandiosity and omnipotence, creating the illusion that we can, and should, have it all. The sense of entitlement, both individual and collective, is pandemic today.

There are many who have become alarmed about the way these messages have been imprinted on our children. That noble but ultimately misguided experiment of the late 1980s and 1990s, the Self-Esteem Movement, is a case in point. It all began in California with a state assemblyman named John Vasconcellos (aka "The Johnny Appleseed of Self-Esteem"), who in 1987 spearheaded the creation of a new curriculum for schoolchildren that added "responsibility, self-respect, and relationship" to the traditional "Three Rs" of elementary education. The idea was to combat the toxic effects of crime, violence, child abuse, chronic welfare, teenage pregnancy, and drug addiction (all fervently believed to result from not loving oneself enough) by inoculating children with "the social vaccine of self-esteem." It was a grand vision.

Raging Entitlement

While the working definition set by the California Task Force to Promote Self-Esteem included such laudable notions as accountability, setting realistic expectations, and respect for others, the sound and sociable core of this retro idealism got lost in the implementation. Some twenty years deeper into the century's now-rampant Me-ism, the part about being responsible and concerned for other people's feelings got lost. In the hands of the grown-up Me Generation, self-esteem for children became equated not with *doing* good but simply with *feeling* good. The character education that had helped to instill such good habits as honesty, helpfulness, and self-control in generations of American children had come to be viewed as too shaming.

In the Era of Self-Esteem, children took their cues from the likes of "Pumsy," an imaginary dragon who urged them to focus within themselves on their own inherent goodness. The operating assumption was that when young people embrace their natural beneficence, they automatically behave in ways that are "personally rewarding" and therefore socially sound. In other words, bad behavior is a product of bad feelings and can be overcome by good thoughts and positive self-affirmations. Everybody wins. Teachers did their part by supplying heavy doses of praise, assurances of specialness, and feed-back that the child was "doing well," even if performance was actu-ally mediocre or poor. Schools were no longer allowed to group children by ability, offer enrichment for gifted students, or encourage competition that might make some feel "less than."

Intentionally or not, we were teaching our children that equal out-come is as much a right as equal opportunity, and that they could ex-pect to be valued and rewarded regardless of what they did or how well they performed. An even more insidious message buried in the subtext was that feeling "bad" is not normal. If your feelings are hurt when you don't get what you want, then something is wrong—you're a victim. Someone or something else is to blame, and you're entitled to recourse. Such thinking is part of the reason today's chil-dren are angrier and more aggressive than previous generations.

Although these attitudes are still deeply embedded in our culture and the messages we give our children, the Self-Esteem Movement has today been widely discredited. For one thing, those three extra "Rs" started to crowd out the original trio, and when the kids had to face the fact that they hadn't mastered the basics, all the affirmations in the world couldn't make them feel really good about themselves. And since hard work and persistence were not part of the package, the road back has been a rocky one. All that hype about specialness has left a trail of popped balloons in its wake, not to mention a land-slide of antisocial behavior, especially as these entitled youngsters have become demanding teens.

Arrogance, Envy, and the Breakdown of Authority

By teaching kids to trust their inner voices before those voices have had a chance to mature, we have also undermined adult authority. Believing they are somehow more pure (un-adult-erated) than their elders conveniently frees us from having to socialize them, but it also deprives us of control when we need it. Children who are left unto themselves, who are taught that objectionable conduct is just being "different" and receive little guidance from parents who are preoccupied with themselves, not surprisingly reject the moral authority of adults to judge them or their behavior—especially when they are constantly exposed to Adults Behaving Badly.

According to the National Center for Education Statistics, the number of high-school principals who complained of serious disciplinary problems rose significantly during the 1990s. Notably, these increases were greater in affluent suburban schools than in the inner city. While verbal abuse of teachers declined in the 1990s by almost 10 percent in the halls of poverty, the trend was in the other direction in affluent and moderate-income schools. A Phi Delta Kappa poll showing a 17 percent increase between 1984 and 1997 of elementary-school teachers who said they had students disrupting class most of the time or fairly often showed that these problems have not been limited to hormonally challenged teens.

The younger generation's lack of respect for adults has a parallel in what might be called the secularization of the spiritual, the rejection of religions that are based on the authority of God in favor of a spirituality that is more pantheistic and self-determined. Notwithstanding an apparent revival of traditional religion in the past few years, from the Age of Aquarius to the more recent New Age movement, the dominant spiritual presence of the late twentieth century has not been God but rather some exalted form of Me.

The narcissistic individual's great difficulty bowing to outside authority may explain the popularity of the kind of spiritualism that emphasizes the deity within, one's own internal "higher power." Whether this represents a pinnacle of moral development (an internalization of the identification with authority) or an exercise in infantile grandiosity varies, of course, among individuals. When that higher power is just Me playing God, it is easy to fool oneself and fall into moral laxity. Such characters demand respect, approval, and admiration from others but don't give the same in return.

Moral Relativism and Shamelessness

The fact that we have become so confused about right and wrong is another sign of the narcissistic times, a reflection of our difficulty functioning as adults. It is as if our collective conscience is not fully formed, and we are caught up in fantasies of grandiosity and omnipotence to protect ourselves from the shame of having to admit our own mistakes.

As a society, we have a lot of trouble with the issue of personal accountability. We tend to think like small children, looking for someone else to blame when things go wrong. Consider how often the most sensational lawsuits are those against a large, powerful industry such as gun manufacturers or tobacco companies. These cultural icons represent the Big Bad Daddies on whom we project our needs for omnipotence. We envy their power, and if we buy a gun or smoke a cigarette, we feel more powerful ourselves. Since our grandiosity tells us that we are entitled to a risk-free world, the Big Bad Daddies are supposed to guarantee our safety even though we know that guns and cigarettes kill. The wounds we suffer when reality intrudes are as much narcissistic as corporeal. We can't bear the shame of lost omnipotence and betrayed grandiosity, and we lash out in a retaliative rage.

Assisting us in these cultural temper tantrums is a Narcissist's dream of a legal system in which gamesmanship bends the truth beyond recognition. If an attorney can make a guilty party appear sympathetic, juries have notoriously been willing to overlook even the most egregious crimes. Particularly effective is the perpetrator-as-victim defense, in which our tendency to justify any behavior on the part of someone who seems victimized (shamed) is exploited.

It may just be that shame has become the ultimate social evil—or so it would seem in a world where values are so relative that violence, corruption, and deceit can be morally distilled to "personal choices." Even when we know that some choices are unacceptable, we look beyond the chooser for someone or something else to blame. Nearly anyone can claim to be some kind of victim, making it difficult to distinguish when real tragedy has occurred and to maintain our sense of compassion for those who truly aren't culpable.

Distortions of Reality: "Image Is Everything"

From political leaders to sports "heroes," from business moguls to entertainment figures, the people who seem best able to evade consequences in today's world are those who can fabricate and project the images we want to see. Manufactured image is one of the pillars of power, and powerful people—along with those who would aspire to power—rely on "spin doctors," agents, publicists, press secretaries, and media consultants to control how we perceive them. We look on with jaded eye, knowing we are being manipulated but enjoying the show. Eventually, reality grows so distorted that we no longer know who or what to believe. We find ourselves in a narcissistic funhouse without a clue what's behind the mirrors. We become mistrustful of our own perceptions, alienated not only from each other but from ourselves as well.

Yet we can't seem to tear ourselves away from the illusions. When image is everything, we lose our appetite for what is real. We stand before a groaning board of pretty puff pastry and think we are about to eat a meal. A proliferation of images without substance stimulates our senses but leaves us spiritually malnourished and craving more. So we return to the buffet again and again. Though they are no more than empty calories, we internalize these images as cultural ideals, and they provide the scripts by which we judge our own worth and that of everything that touches our lives. It is through them that we come to know what is beautiful, what is good, what is desirable, and what has meaning.

The power of images is an extremely seductive force. Ask the 1,840 American girls under the age of nineteen who had breast augmentation surgery in 1998 (up 57 percent from 1996 and 89 percent from 1992). The majority of these teens raided their college funds for cosmetic reasons alone and "to feel better about themselves," many of them encouraged by mothers who had also been surgically altered to more closely resemble the cultural ideal. You may question their values or their youthful impatience, but you can't argue with the fact that, even in this postfeminist era, large breasts can still give a woman a measure of power.

As real authority has eroded, we sense that image manipulation is the way to get what we want. The sad truth for all of us is that in a world where falseness is a given, these are the strategies that work.

When Competition Becomes Exploitation

Flooded as we are with images that arouse and tempt us in every imaginable way, it is only natural that we should want to have what we see. The more pervasive the images, the more demand is created, and from the perception that supply is limited, competition is born.

There is nothing intrinsically evil about competition; in fact, quite the opposite is true. We are all programmed with an aggressive instinct to fight, if necessary, for what we want and need. Competitive aggression, the kind in which two or more people apply energy toward a goal that cannot be shared, is a healthy striving that ends when, win or lose, the competition is resolved. In optimal circumstances, both winner and loser benefit from the struggle and can feel a sense of satisfaction in having participated and given their best effort.

Perhaps the reason that competitive aggression has gotten such a bad rap in recent decades is that, too often, it doesn't end when the competition is over. There is something else going on, a meta playing field where one's very worth as a human being is at stake. We're all familiar with the ugly side of victory, with gloating winners not content with having prevailed until they can further humiliate the losers. This is not healthy aggression but exploitation and annihilation, the acting out of narcissistic rage. When it dominates the scene, competition becomes a dirty word.

The hallmarks of cultural narcissism are deeply woven into the fabric of our current society, the environment in which we love and fight, work and play, nurture and teach our children. For some time now, we have given unhealthy narcissism a place to grow. If we are to redeem ourselves, and future generations, we need to resist these forces, fighting for the principles of self-awareness and self-control, reality, good boundaries, and reciprocity wherever we encounter the Seven Deadly Sins. It's a big job, and it begins at home.

20

Becoming Better Parents

RECENTLY, A ROPER NATIONAL YOUTH SURVEY asked teenagers what they thought was wrong with America today. They were given fifteen options to choose from, and these were their top four choices: selfishness/people not thinking of the rights of others (56 percent), people who don't respect the law and the authorities (52 percent), wrongdoing by politicians (48 percent), and lack of parental discipline of children and teens (47 percent). The young people, it seems, are well aware of the narcissism that floods our world.

Most of the narcissism in turn-of-the-century American society is a product of two things: cultural influences and faulty parenting. The two are closely linked. When the baby boomers threw off the shackles of traditional values as repressive and unenlightened and the point of reference became peers who were trying to reinvent parenting to suit their own self-centered needs, what we got was a whole lot of people justifying choices that had less to do with what was good, or even good enough, for children than with what fulfilled parents as individuals. In the pursuit of their own happiness, too many parents have indulged in grandiosity, omnipotence, envy, and perfectionism, ignoring the separate needs of their children and misunderstanding or misreading the developmental underpinnings of their sometimes challenging behavior.

Look around. Do you know parents who:

- Have unrealistic expectations of their children?
- Micromanage their children's lives without regard for their feelings and wishes?
- Live through their children?
- Use their children to meet their own needs?
- Infect their children with their fears and anxieties?
- Treat their children as friends or confidants?
- Put their children in the middle of conflicts with the other parent?

How about parents who are:

- Overly controlling?
- Intrusive?
- Sexually suggestive or coarse in a child's presence?
- So busy with their own lives that they can't participate in their children's?

Two narcissistic conceits have governed our journey to the current culture of narcissism. One is that I can have it all—and should. The other is that no one should be allowed to interfere with my pursuit of happiness and self-fulfillment. These two notions have clearly found their way into modern parenting practices, ensuring that the Seven Deadly Sins of Narcissism will be with us for some time to come.

Seven Parental Attitudes That Create Narcissistic Children

1. My child is special and deserves to have everything, every experience, and every advantage. If I can't provide it, society should.

The word "special" has lost its meaning in today's world. It used to mean possessed of some *unusual* quality or *superior* in some way. Now, many people view feeling special as an intrinsic part of self-esteem and expect, as a matter of routine, to be made to feel special by others. "I didn't feel special," we hear people say, as if they were somehow gypped. This is narcissistic entitlement, and it is an unconscious and pervasive part of the way we have come to think.

Certainly, every child is special to his or her parents, or we hope that they are. Children are also unique persons and entitled to be treated with kindness and respect for their individuality. But there is no reason others should regard my child as "special" just because I do. That attitude is rooted in a narcissistic failure to recognize that others are separate and not obliged to think and feel exactly as we do.

In America, children are entitled to protection from abuse and neglect, and to a free public education. There are many, many other things that we would like children to have, but it pretty much falls on their parents, or the generosity of others, to provide these things. They are not entitlements. It may indeed "take a village" to raise a child, in the sense that the larger community and society have an investment in that child's welfare and healthy development, but children are first and foremost the responsibility of the people who bring them into the world or those who legally adopt or care for them. Most parents expect to provide for their children, even if they have to make sacrifices to do it. Unfortunately, not all parents share this sense of responsibility.

The child—or adult—who expects to be treated as special is doomed to a lifetime of disappointment and relationship problems when others fail to reflect his or her unreal self-image.

   2. My child should never suffer. (If my child is unhappy, I
      am a bad parent.) Failure is always a negative experience
      and should be avoided at all costs.

Let's face it: Suffering is part of the human condition. As much as we would like to shield children from pain, sometimes things happen that are outside our control. Sometimes these things are of tragic proportion, such as disease, disaster, and even death. Yet most of the time they are very ordinary, such as losing in competition or not getting to have the latest fad toy. Parents today turn themselves inside out to spare their children sufferings both large and small. One has only to look at the frenzied demand for particular toy items during the holiday season, or the pressure to keep up with the latest fads in kiddie culture. But these parents are missing an important point when they put themselves through such extraordinary hoops. Children, like adults, can be helped to face life's disappointments or even crises and to become stronger for having done so. With good parental support, obstacles and even failures are what build character.

Feeling tender-hearted toward one's child is a good quality, but sometimes what makes it difficult for parents to tolerate a child's suffering is that the parent feels it is happening to him or her. Our pain is not our children's pain but rather something that may have been triggered by overidentification with the child. This is harmful in two ways: One, it takes away from the child's experience by making it "all about me" and depriving the child of empathic support at a time of distress, and two, we sometimes go too far to "control away" the pain we cannot tolerate. If we cannot tolerate our children's pain, we risk creating an unreal world of indulgence and anxious overcontrol. Not only does the child come to believe in entitlement to that unreal world, but he or she also misses opportunities to master distress.

These are the children who become "entitlement monsters," and those tantrums we see are not just bad behavior, they represent a genuine lack of skill in responding to the day-to-day obstacles of life. Children need opportunities to master feelings of frustration, loss, disappointment, loneliness, boredom, envy, guilt, and anger—and help doing so from compassionate, available adults. They need experiences that give them a realistic sense of themselves in the world: winners and losers, good and bad, self-reliant and dependent, givers and takers, assertive and compassionate.

3. What's good for me is good for my child. If the sacrifices I make for my child interfere with my self-actualization, my unhappiness will be worse for my child than if I didn't make sacrifices in the first place.

This attitude is rooted in a parent's failure to see the separateness of his or her child. The more difficult truth is that parents' and children's needs are often very different, competing, and even mutually exclusive. Parents of the 1970s, 1980s, and 1990s sometimes made choices that were good for them but very traumatic for their children. Divorces that might have been prevented left children estranged from one or both parents, in the middle of parental conflict and custody disputes, and with a series of quasi or would-be stepparents who moved into and out of their lives, wreaking havoc on the child's sense of secure attachment. Parents indulged in chemical dependency and other addictive or compulsive behavior that made them emotionally unavailable or worse. Parents pursued careers or lifestyles that subjected children to prolonged parental absences and inconsistent caretaking. Sometimes, these choices were necessary, but sometimes they were merely self-indulgent, without regard for the real impact on children. "What's good for me is good for my child" became a way of thinking that dismissed children's separate needs and interests and prevented adequate support for the children. This attitude is no different from putting on blinders or looking the other way when one's own child is suffering.

This contributes to prolonged narcissism in children by blurring boundaries and forcing children to rely on their own underdeveloped resources in times of stress. These are often the children who "raise themselves" and are left with a combination of unresolved omnipotence, profoundly conflicted dependency needs, anger, or difficulty trusting others.

While it is undoubtedly true that children are better off with happy parents than with unhappy ones, what is best for children is when parents can find happiness in being parents.

4. Children need freedom of expression. Their spirits are "pure," and without adult interference, they will naturally blossom into superior beings. There's no use trying to stop problem behavior by being authoritarian. That just alienates kids by shaming them needlessly.

Nobody likes to be the bad guy, especially with his or her own child. But belief in the purity of "the natural child" is a narcissistic distortion of reality that conveniently lets the parent off the hook for socializing a child to become a functioning member of society. Children deprived of parental instruction do not usually evolve into "good" people; instead, they are more likely to have behavioral problems— and possibly unresolved infantile narcissism.

A Mind of His Own

"Someone ought to teach that kid to get along," was the buzz around the teachers' lounge when word got out that eight-year-old Johnny had started another ruckus on the playground. They all felt pretty sorry for Ruth,

Johnny's teacher, who kept having to explain to various parents why their kids were coming home with torn clothes, bruises, and the occasional bloody nose. Ruth had had problem kids before, but never one like Johnny—trouble just seemed to erupt all around him whenever the class had free time.

Ruth had tried talking to Johnny, but she couldn't get through. He always had an explanation about why he was right and someone else was wrong. He seemed to expect other kids to do things his way, and when they resisted he would become haughty and provocative. He was utterly lacking in the routine skills of give-and-take.

So Ruth called a conference with Johnny's parents. Frankly, she was a little surprised that she hadn't heard from them—Johnny seldom came out of the fray unscathed and had taken home a few nicks and bumps of his own. But when she finally sat down with them face to face, they seemed totally unfazed by the tales of their son's behavior.

"We've always taught Johnny to fight his own battles," said Johnny's mother, Kris. Indeed, thought Ruth, beginning to see the larger problem. "Johnny's always had a mind of his own," his father, Greg, chimed in. The pride in his voice was not lost on Ruth. "Yes," she answered carefully, "Johnny is certainly very sure of himself, and he has no problems expressing what he wants." Kris and Greg beamed at each other. "However," Ruth continued, "Johnny does seem to have some difficulty hearing what others want, and also, I'm afraid, respecting how they feel. He becomes quite aggressive when he doesn't get his way." She braced herself, expecting to see an adult version of Johnny's now-familiar temper. "They're just kids," said Kris, shrugging, "and kids fight. If you leave them alone, they'll work it out. That's how we handle it at home, and it works for us!"

Children need parental input to get through early childhood narcissism. They need help in having their infantile omnipotence and grandiosity deflated, and in regulating the shame that comes with having the bubble of narcissism popped. They need strong, nurturing parental figures who can serve as models for idealization. They need corrective feedback about what parents believe to be right and true and important. They need parents who have self-control and who practice what they preach.

It is by internalizing the values of an idealized parent that children develop conscience. If we wish our children to know right from wrong, we not only have to teach them, but also have to be people they can admire.

5. Empathy for a child is the same as treating him or her as a friend, sharing all my feelings and "modeling" closeness. Being honest means telling a child whatever I'm thinking or feeling and disclosing any dirty laundry from my past or any problems I'm having now. Children need to know the truth about their parents at all times.

The Little Grown-Up

Tina's mother likes to tell people her daughter was "born strong." To Mom, Tina is someone she can count on to help around the house and to look after the younger children when she feels like retiring to her bedroom with the curtains drawn. Tina seems wise beyond her years, and when Mom feels depressed, as she often does, the ten-year-old is such a comfort. She even understands why Mom is unhappy with Dad.

Tina feels sad for her mother, but she adores her father and has a special place in his life, too. The two of them are a team, taking care of business, taking care of Mom. Tina and her father shop together, cook together, and Sundays are their day to play cards together, just the two of them. Like Mom, Dad turns to Tina as a confidante. She knows his sorrows and his aggravations, and secretly, she is on his side.

Tina was known even in kindergarten as "the little girl who uses big words." Since then, she has been a top student and usually the teacher's pet. So when she began acting defiant in class and talking back at home, every-

one was surprised. Her parents figure she must be starting puberty a little ahead of schedule.

Empathy for a child is based on an understanding of that child's real needs and capacities at each stage of development, as well as an intuitive feel for the child's unique rhythms and idiosyncracies and a realistic assessment of what the child can handle at any given time. It is also based on caring enough to maintain good parental boundaries.

Good parental boundaries mean not treating a child as a friend, confidant, or confessor. While such treatment may indeed make a child feel "special," it is the wrong kind of specialness. It communicates to a child that he or she is an equal, and that the parent and child roles have been obscured. Parents who indulge in this kind of behavior with their children are often surprised when their children have little or no respect for authority, either the parent's or that of any other adult. This is because they have been allowed to share in what they perceive as the parent's grandiosity and omnipotence at the expense of developing a real Self. Although it may be difficult for a warm and caring adult to see how this is inappropriate, children often experience this kind of chumminess as intrusive as well as inappropriately gratifying. Once again, it is more about what the parent needs than what is good for the child, and it is by no means harmless

6. Sex is natural, and children should not be made to feel shameful about their sexuality by adults behaving in "repressed" ways.

The Family That Plays Together . . .

It is a holiday weekend at the cineplex, and a matinee showing of a highly publicized PG-13 movie has drawn a crowd of about sixty, approximately a quarter of whom are children under the age of ten accompanied by their parents. A family of four has settled into a back row, passing the popcorn and soft drinks, enjoying some quality time together. In the opening sequence of the movie, a man and a woman in bed are engaged in a little après-sex talk when the woman disengages herself, starts to behave oddly, and then suddenly turns into a malevolent "she-bot." As semiautomatic bullets spray from her nipples and her face falls off to reveal her cyborg circuitry, the little girl in the back row shrieks, "Mommy, it's too scary!" "No, it's not," her mother replies, and the child falls silent. Pass the popcorn.

The movie, as it turns out, is one long sexual intercourse joke, with pantomiming of perverse sexual acts, crude references to body parts and bodily functions, and an assortment of characters demonstrating various coital positions as they hop into and out of bed with one another, all in ribald humor. The children in the theater grow restless and noisy, but no one—not one family—leaves.

Parents since the 1970s have put a lot of stock in modeling behavior that they want to instill in their children. This is perhaps nowhere more misguided than in the overexposure of children to sexual stimulation that they are developmentally unprepared to handle.

Sometimes children are overstimulated as a result of the deluge of sexual material in our culture. It is a symptom of our narcissistic times that adult cravings for sexual stimulation are so blatantly allowed to undermine a wholesome environment for children. Concerned parents must guard against the tendency to feel overwhelmed and confused by, or indifferent to, these influences. Even if you cannot fully protect your child from sexual overstimulation (and you can't), your willingness to try creates a kind of boundary that children can internalize as a self-protective barrier. Children need all the protection we can offer from that which they are developmentally unready to handle.

Certainly, parents should model adult love and affection and should answer questions about sex and reproduction in a straightforward manner that is appropriate to the child's ability to understand. And certainly, children's spontaneous sexuality should be treated as natural. But children do sometimes have sexual feelings and are subject to being stimulated by parental nudity, overt sexual behavior or even innuendo, and intrusive information of a sexual nature. What is natural for healthy, loving adults may be too much for children, and this is not so much a problem to be overcome in the interests of eradicating "repression" as a reality to be respected for the sake of preserving a child's sexual and emotional health.

The sexual overstimulation of children by what they see or hear in the home is a form of emotional incest, and it can be just as damaging as physical incest and even more difficult to recall and work through as an adult because there was not so much a traumatic event as a climate of unclear boundaries that gratified the parent in some way at the expense of the child. These children often become sexually precocious or may masturbate in public as a way of expressing the blurred boundaries they feel.

7. The way to build self-esteem is to tell children how "special" they are and to have them recite "affirmations" on a regular basis. Children shouldn't have to accomplish anything in order to believe in themselves, and they should be spared the harmful effects of competition.

Where does confidence come from? Does it come from telling yourself that you are able to do something, or from taking the risk to try and finding out what you really can do?

Self-esteem works the same way. When children are encouraged to make an effort, they discover their own competence and have an experience of mastery that becomes part of how they see themselves. If they stumble or fail along the way, that too is a learning experience that has the potential to help them become stronger and more realistic about themselves. Not everyone can be good at everything, but finding out what you *are* good at is part of forming a positive identity.

Parents can help by creating an environment in which opportunities are offered, effort is valued, and children are given skills for handling disappointment.

It is important to reflect back to a child an accurate perception of that child's true Self. Children are not fooled when we tell them they are special and they have done nothing to merit that accolade in their own or anyone else's eyes. But children do buy into our expectation that they *be* special by clinging to their infantile grandiosity and omnipotence. Hollow affirmations only reinforce narcissism in children at the expense of their developing a real Self.

In addition to love, all children need these things, from birth to emancipation: consistency, structure, good boundaries, empathic attunement, and *someone to be an adult.* They need to know who is in their family and who is not, what place or places they can call home, where and when they are supposed to eat and sleep, what are the rules of conduct of the household and to whom they apply (roles and responsibilities), what belongs to them and what does not. They need to be taught what their own personal boundaries are, who can violate them, and under what circumstances. They need to understand also that others have personal boundaries that need to be respected. They need to know whom they can depend on to meet each of their needs: who will comfort them when they are hurt or sick or frightened, who will protect them when they are in danger, who will provide them with the necessities of life, who will teach them what they need to know to become more self-reliant. The sum total of these "knowings" constitute the boundaries of their lives.

As parents, it is our job to set these structures in place and to maintain or alter them over time. It goes without saying that we will have a great deal of difficulty doing this for our children if we also have trouble doing it for ourselves. If your life is in chaos, you will need to figure out why and go about setting it straight. To the extent that you are able to be in control, you will need to set boundaries around the things that affect you and the ways you interact with other people. You will need to be a parent while you do this, and let your children be children. That is what is meant by good generational boundaries.

If you are a parent, you can help prevent narcissism—one child at a time.

Introduction
xv   Back in the mid-1970s, the sociologist Christopher Lasch:
Lasch, C. (1978). *The culture of narcissism.* New York: Norton.

Chapter 1
5   Recent research in neurobiology has shown: Schore, A. N.
(1994). *Affect regulation and the origin of the self: The neurobiology of
emotional development.* Hillsdale, N.J.: Erlbaum, 241.

Chapter 2
8   These so-called closet Narcissists: Masterson, J. F. (1993). *The
emerging self: A developmental, self, and object relations approach to the
treatment of the closet narcissistic disorder of the self.* New York:
Brunner/Mazel.

Chapter 5
21   The child's normal narcissistic rages: Schore, A. N. (1994). *Affect regulation and the origin of the self: The neurobiology of emotional
development.* Hillsdale, N.J.: Erlbaum, 339–41.

Chapter 6
24   Children aged ten to fourteen months have been observed:
Schore, A. N. (1994). *Affect regulation and the origin of the self: The
neurobiology of emotional development.* Hillsdale, N.J.: Erlbaum,
350–51.

Chapter 7

28 It is one of the jobs of parents: White, B. (1985). *The first three years of life.* Englewood Cliffs, N.J.: Prentice-Hall, 181.

30 The American Psychiatric Association estimates that: American Psychiatric Association. (1994). *Diagnostic and statistical manual of mental disorders,* 4th ed. DSM-IV. Washington, D.C.: American Psychiatric Association, 658–61.

Chapter 8

35 what psychologists call "the process of separation-individuation": Mahler, M. S. (1986). On human symbiosis and the vicissitudes of individuation. In P. Buckley (ed.), *Essential papers on object relations.* New York: New York University Press, 200–21 (original work published in 1968).

36 It was nearly a century ago when Sigmund Freud: Freud, S. (1955). Beyond the pleasure principle. In *The standard edition of the complete psychological works of Sigmund Freud.* London: Hogarth Press (original work published 1920).

36 We now know that even very young babies want: Stern, D. N. (1985). *The interpersonal world of the infant: A view from psychoanalysis and developmental psychology.* New York: Basic Books.

40 Brain research on infants has shown that: Schore, A. N. (1994). *Affect regulation and the origin of the self: The neurobiology of emotional development.* Hillsdale, N.J.: Erlbaum, 24.

40 This "low-keyedness," however, is normal: Ibid., 227.

41 The experience of elation, shame, and recovery then becomes: Izard, C. E. (1991). *The psychology of emotions.* New York: Plenum.

41 They need to learn that they are unique and important: White, B. (1985). *The first three years of life.* Englewood Cliffs, N.J.: Prentice-Hall, 181.

Chapter 9

56 Researchers have shown that mothers: Speers, R. W., and

D. C. Morter (1980). Overindividuation and underseparation in the pseudomature child. In R. F. Lax, S. Bach, and J. A. Burland (eds.), *Rapprochement: The critical subphase of separation-individuation.* Northvale, N.J.: Jason Aronson, 457–77.

Chapter 14

90 Puberty begins when a part of the brain: Berger, K. S. (2001). *The developing person through the life span,* 5th ed. New York: Worth, 382–87.

91 At the same time that all these physical and emotional changes are taking place: Ibid., 407–16.

94–95 the tenfold increase in depression in the United States: Lewinsohn, P. M., et al. (1994). Major depression in community adolescents: Age of onset, episode duration, and time to recurrence. *Journal of the American Academy of Child and Adolescent Psychiatry,* 33(6): 809–18.

95 The essential task of adolescence: Erikson, E. (1963). *Childhood and society,* 2d rev. ed. New York: Norton.

95 the severing of infantile ties of dependence: Blos, P. (1968). Character formation in adolescence. *The Psychoanalytic Study of the Child,* 23: 245–63.

95 Psychoanalytic thinkers find a remarkable resemblance: Esman, A. H. (1980). Adolescent psychopathology and the rapprochement process. In R. F. Lax, S. Bach, and J. A. Burland (eds.), *Rapprochement: The critical subphase of separation-individuation.* Northvale, N.J.: Jason Aronson.

96 a psychic restructuring is underway: Blos, P. (1968). Character formation in adolescence. *The Psychoanalytic Study of the Child,* 23: 252.

96 There are basically three things that can happen: Berger, K. S. (2001). *The developing person through the life span,* 5th ed. New York: Worth, 436.

98   From 1978 to 1998, the percentage of American families:
Kantrowitz, B., and P. Wingert (1999, May 10). How well do you
know your kid? *Newsweek,* 36–40.

99   "parents spend 40 percent less time with their kids": Cloud, J.
(1999, May 31). Just a routine school shooting. *Time,* 34–43.

99   *Newsweek* chimed in: Kantrowitz, B., and P. Wingert. (1999,
May 10). How well do you know your kid? *Newsweek,* 36.

99   a study of elementary-school-aged boys: Dodge, K. A., and
D. R. Somberg (1987). Hostile attributional biases among aggressive
boys are exacerbated under conditions of threat to self. *Child Development,* 58: 213–24.

99   future antisocial behavior could be predicted: Glueck, E. T.,
and S. Glueck (1966). Identification of potential delinquents at 2–3
years of age. *International Journal of Social Psychiatry,* 12: 5–16.

Chapter 15

110 When the child is deprived of empathic care: Schore, A. N.
(1994). *Affect regulation and the origin of the self: The neurobiology of
emotional development.* Hillsdale, N.J.: Erlbaum, 403–404.

110 These individuals may turn to chemical substances as "auxiliary regulators": Wurmser, L. (1987). "Flight from conscience: Experiences with the psychoanalytic treatment of compulsive drug
abusers, Part Two: Dynamic and therapeutic conclusions from the
experiences with psychoanalysis of drug users." *Journal of Substance
Abuse Treatment,* 4: 169–174.

110 The drugs act to trigger narcissistic fantasies: Ulman, R. B. &
Paul, H. (1989). "A self-psychological theory and approach to treating substance abuse disorders: The 'intersubjective absorption' hypothesis.". In A. Goldberg (Ed.), *Progress in self psychology,* Vol. 6.
Hillsdale, N.J.: The Analytic Press, 129–156.

111 Parents who are inconsistent: Wurmser, L. (1974). "Psychoanalytic considerations of the etiology of compulsive drug use." *American Psychoanalytic Association Journal,* 22: 820–843.

111 Anything short of total union: Ibid., 833.

111 Like Narcissists, people who turn to drugs: Yorke, C. (1970). "A critical review of some psychoanalytic literature on drug addiction." *British Journal of Medical Psychology,* 43: 141–159.

112 Both addicts and Narcissists are impatient people: Wilson, A., Passik, S. D., Faude, J., Abrams, J., and Gordon, E. (1989). "A hierarchical model of opiate addiction: Failures of self-regulation as a central aspect of substance abuse." *Journal of Nervous and Mental Disease,* 177: 390–399.

112 they seek, through drugs, to alleviate their anxieties about their own competence: Fenichel, O. (1945).*The psychoanalytic theory of neurosis..* New York: W. W. Norton.

112 Childlike magical thinking may make drugs seem seductive, promising relief without the need for active mastery and adaptation: Jacobson, E. (1961). "Adolescent moods and the remodeling of psychic structures in adolescence." T*he Psychoanalytic Study of the Child ,* 16: 164–183.

113 From 1991 to 1996, current (within the previous month) illicit drug use: Office of National Drug Control Policy (1999). *National Drug Control Strategy*. Washington, DC, 18–23.

113 Noting that addicts often referred to their drug of choice as "mood food" or "instant Mommy,": Wieder, H. and Kaplan, E. H. (1969). "Drug use in adolescents: Psychodynamic meaning and pharmacogenic effect." *The Psychoanalytic Study of the Child,* 24: 399–431.

114 The state of opium intoxication known as "being on the nod": Ibid.

115 Certain individuals may use cocaine—the drug of choice for grandiose Narcissists: Khantzian, E. J. (1985). "The self-medication hypothesis of addictive disorders: Focus on heroin and cocaine dependence." *The American Journal of Psychiatry,* 142: 1259–1264.

115 Of all the types of regressive gratifications provided by drugs: Wurmser, L. (1974). "Psychoanalytic considerations of the etiology of compulsive drug use." *American Psychoanalytic Association Journal,* 22: 839.

115 The vast majority of alcohol and drug use in our culture is of an experimental, casual, or recreational nature: Ibid., 822.

115 In addition to alcohol, drugs, and food, we can also be addicted to . . .: Bradshaw, J. (1988). Healing the shame that binds you. Deerfield Beach, Florida: Health Communications, Inc., 95–96.

116 Otto Kernberg, who gave us much of what we know about pathological narcissism: Kernberg, O. (1990). *Borderline conditions and pathological narcissism*. Northvale, N. J: Jason Aronson. (Original work published 1975), 222.

Chapter 16
122 the obliteration of one partner's autonomy in the service: To the narcissist, the "narcissistically cathected object" is "someone at their disposal who can be used as an echo, who can be controlled, is completely centered on them, will never desert them, and offers full attention and admiration." Miller, A. (1986). Depression and grandiosity as related forms of narcissistic disturbances. In A. P. Morrison (ed.), *Essential papers on narcissism*. New York: University Press, 326–27.

122 The resulting "undifferentiated ego mass": Bowen, M. A. (1960). Family concept of schizophrenia. In D. D. Jackson (ed.), *The etiology of schizophrenia*. New York: Basic Books.

122 The person who submits to the tyranny of a Narcissist: Ethel

Person wrote: "The impulse to merge may be debased into a different kind of surrender—one in which the lover seeks to submerge
his identity into that of the Other . . . the lover is seeking not so
much to transcend the self as he is to bolster the self, to make up for
what he experiences as lacunae in his own personality." Person, E. S.
(1988). *Dreams of love and fateful encounters: The power of romantic
passion.* New York: Penguin, 138.

123 There is an element of altruism in healthy love: Kernberg, O.
(1995). *Love relations: Normality and pathology.* New Haven, Conn.:
Yale University Press, 146.

123 a fantasy "twinship": Ibid., 154.

125 Whatever Narcissists admire in a loved one: Ibid., 151.

128 the Narcissist becomes enraged when the pipeline: Ethel
Person wrote: "Acording to H. Kohut (1971), an object is narcissistically cathected when we experience it not as the centre of its own
activity but as part of ourselves. If the object does not behave in the
way in which we expect or wish, we may at times be immeasurably
disappointed or offended, almost as if an arm ceased to obey us, or a
function that we take for granted (such as memory) lets us down.
This sudden loss of control can also lead to intense narcissistic rage."
Person, E. S. (1988). *Dreams of love and fateful encounters: The power
of romantic passion.* New York: Penguin, 323–24.

128 a full range of every sexual dysfunction: Kernberg, op. cit.,
153–55.

130 stable relationships with partners they consider to be "the very
best.": Ibid., 156.

131 The closet Narcissist is an unassuming type: Masterson, J. F.
(1993). *The emerging self: A developmental, self, and object relations approach to the treatment of the closet narcissistic disorder of the self.* New
York: Brunner/Mazel.

131 to inflate herself via osmosis: Ethel Person wrote: "A subtle
power modality . . . is that which is disguised as caretaking. Some

lovers are extremely nurturant in order to disguise their underlying and unacceptable feelings of dependency . . . this sometimes camouflages a conscious condescension or disparagement of the beloved. More often, however, it masks a profound identification with the beloved's dependency wishes." Person, E. S. (1988). *Dreams of love and fateful encounters: The power of romantic passion.* New York: Penguin, 176.

133 way stations on our journey to more mature love: For an interesting perspective on how narcissistic wounds can be healed through couple therapy, see: Solomon, M. F. (1989). *Narcissism and intimacy: Love and marriage in an age of confusion.* New York: Norton.

134 Each of the developmental dramas in the Birth of Me: Ethel Person wrote: "From the psychoanalytic perspective, the successful achievement of mature love depends on the lover's having been able to negotiate certain prior experiences successfully; otherwise, his capacity to fall in love will be sorely limited." Person, E. S. (1988). *Dreams of love and fateful encounters: The power of romantic passion.* New York: Penguin, 91.

138 When two very self-absorbed people find themselves: Ethel Person wrote: "In self-aggrandizing love (or vanity-love), the lover forms an attachment in large part as a means to an end, either to achieve some specific gain like money, a less tangible one like social advantage, or to prop up his vanity or ego." Also, "Neurotic love, analogous to vanity-love, seeks to satisfy a real need, but not the same kind of need that is met by mutual, reciprocal love. Many neurotic attachments are based on dependency needs or the fear of being alone." Ibid., 52–54.

139 True reciprocity also requires mutual trust: Ethel Person wrote: "Falling in love—and the ultimate achievement of genuine love—requires an ability to trust oneself as well as the Other, to reveal one's weaknesses and foibles and risk becoming the object of fear and hatred, of condescension, humiliation, or rejection." Ibid., 44.

139 a partner who is not a Narcissist: Ethel Person wrote: "Individuals best able to maintain the paradoxical stance required in love—the ability to achieve union without compromising autonomy, and to tolerate aloneness without collapse of the self—are often those with a strong sense of self." Ibid., 328.

Chapter 17
158 Many of these coping strategies, adapted from: Greene, R., and J. Elffers (1998). *The 48 laws of power.* New York: Viking.

Chapter 18
168 Personality theorist Otto Kernberg called "malignant": Kernberg, O. (1984). *Severe personality disorders.* New Haven, Conn.: Yale University Press.

168 who so idealize their own aggressive power: Rosenfeld, H. (1971). Theory of life and death instincts: Aggressive aspects of narcissism. *International Journal of Psycho-Analysis,* 45: 332–37.

170 master the art of "noncombative firmness" and practice "bland indifference": Golomb, E. (1992). *Trapped in the mirror: Adult children of narcissists in their struggle for self.* New York: Quill/William Morrow.

Chapter 19
179 According to the National Center for Education Statistics: Hymowitz, K. S. (1999, December 9). Suburban kids at risk. *Los Angeles Times,* B11. All of the statistics in this paragraph are from Hymowitz, author of *Ready or not, why treating children as adults endangers their future—and ours.* New York: Free Press, 1999.

181 the 1,840 American girls under the age of nineteen who had: Warren, P. M. (1999, May 21). A cap and gown—and new breasts. *Los Angeles Times,* E1.

Chapter 20
185 Survey asked teenagers what they thought: Moore, B. (1999, January 20). The trouble with adults today. *Los Angeles Times,* E1-4.

SUGGESTED READINGS

Affect Regulation and the Origin of the Self: The Neurobiology of Emotional Development. Allan N. Schore. Hillsdale, N.J.: Lawrence Erlbaum Associates, 1994.

Borderline Conditions and Pathological Narcissism. Otto Kernberg. Northvale, N.J.: Jason Aronson, 1990.

Childhood and Society. Erik Erikson. New York: W. W. Norton, 1963.

Children of the Self-Absorbed: A Grown-Up's Guide to Getting Over Narcissistic Parents. Nina W. Brown. Oakland, Calif.: New Harbinger, 2001.

The Culture of Narcissism. Christopher Lasch. New York: W. W. Norton, 1978.

The Destructive Narcissistic Pattern. Nina W. Brown. Westport, Conn.: Praeger, 1998.

The Drama of the Gifted Child: The Search for the True Self. Alice Miller. New York: HarperCollins, 1996.

Dreams of Love and Fateful Encounters: The Power of Romantic Passion. Ethel S. Person. New York: Penguin Books, 1988.

The Emerging Self: A Developmental, Self, and Object Relations Approach to the Treatment of the Closet Narcissistic Disorder of the Self. James F. Masterson. New York: Brunner/Mazel, 1993.

Facing Shame: Families in Recovery. Merle A. Fossum and Marilyn J. Mason. New York: W. W. Norton, 1986.

The Feel-Good Curriculum: The Dumbing-Down of America's Kids in the Name of Self-Esteem. Maureen Stout. Boston: Perseus Books, 2000.

Suggested Readings

The 48 Laws of Power. Robert Greene and Joost Elffers. New York: Viking, 1998.

Healing the Shame That Binds You. John Bradshaw. DeerfieldBeach, FL: Health Communications, Inc., 1988.

The Interpersonal World of the Infant: A View From Psychoanalysis and Developmental Psychology. Daniel N. Stern. New York: Basic Books, 1985.

Love Relations: Normality and Pathology. Otto Kernberg. New Haven, Conn.: Yale University Press, 1995.

Narcissism: Denial of the True Self. Alexander Lowen. New York: Touchstone/Simon & Schuster, 1997.

Narcissism and Intimacy: Love and Marriage in an Age of Confusion. Marion F. Solomon. New York: W. W. Norton, 1989.

The Narcissistic Family: Diagnosis and Treatment. Stephanie Donaldson-Pressman and Robert M. Pressman. New York: Lexington Books, 1994.

On Adolescence: A Psychoanalytic Interpretation. Peter Blos. New York: Free Press, 1962.

Personality Disorders in Older Adults: Emerging Issues in Diagnosis and Treatment. Erlene Rosowsky, Robert C. Adams, and Richard A. Zweig, eds., Mahwah, N.J.: Lawrence Erlbaum Associates, 1999.

The Search for the Real Self: Unmasking the Personality Disorders of Our Age. James F. Masterson. New York: Free Press, 1988.

Shame: The Underside of Narcissism. Andrew P. Morrison. Hillsdale, N.J.: Analytic Press, 1989.

Toxic Coworkers: How to Deal With Dysfunctional People on the Job. Allan A. Cavaiola and Neil J. Lavender. Oakland, Calif.: New Harbinger, 2000.

Trapped in the Mirror: Adult Children of Narcissists in Their Struggle for Self. Elan Golomb. New York: Quill/William Morrow, 1992.

INDEX

Sandy Hotchkiss, LCSW, maintains a private practice in individual, couple, and family therapy in Pasadena, California. She is an active member of the California Society for Clinical Social Work and has taught in the Master's Program in Social Work at the Univeristy of Southern California.